CONTOURLINES

CONTOURLINES

NEW RESPONSES TO LANDSCAPE IN WORD AND IMAGE

EDITED BY NEIL WENBORN
AND M. E. J. HUGHES

MAGDALENE COLLEGE
PUBLICATIONS

SALT

CAMBRIDGE

PUBLISHED BY SALT PUBLISHING
Fourth Floor, 2 Tavistock Place, Bloomsbury, London WC1H 9RA United Kingdom

IN ASSOCIATION WITH MAGDALENE COLLEGE PUBLICATIONS

All rights reserved

Selection and introduction © Neil Wenborn and M.E.J. Hughes, 2009
Individual contributions © the contributors, 2009

The right of Neil Wenborn and M.E.J. Hughes to be identified as
the editors of this work has been asserted by them in accordance
with Section 77 of the Copyright, Designs and Patents Act 1988.

This book is in copyright. Subject to statutory exception
and to provisions of relevant collective licensing agreements,
no reproduction of any part may take place without the written
permission of Salt Publishing.

Salt Publishing 2009

Printed and bound in the United Kingdom by Butler Tanner & Dennis Ltd.

Typeset in Bembo 11/14

This book is sold subject to the conditions that it shall not,
by way of trade or otherwise, be lent, re-sold, hired out,
or otherwise circulated without the publisher's prior consent
in any form of binding or cover other than that in which
it is published and without a similar condition including this
condition being imposed on the subsequent purchaser.

ISBN 978 1 84471 715 6 hardback

1 3 5 7 9 8 6 4 2

CONTENTS

PREFACE	ix
INTRODUCTION	xi
RUTH PADEL	
THE TREASURE MAP	1
TONY CURTIS	
LYDSTEP HEADLAND	2
PHILIP GROSS	
BETWEENLAND	4
TONY CURTIS	
TWO AT MANORBIER	13
SUSAN WICKS	
INSIDE THE MOVEMENT	14
JANE ROUTH	
AN UNSPOKEN RULE ABOUT DISTANCES	15
THE ORCHID FIELD	17
JOHN GREENING	
A HUNTINGDONSHIRE ELEGY	20
TONY CURTIS	
REACHING YR ACHUB	21
NEIL WENBORN	
DOVER	22
RICHARD BERENGARTEN	
APPROACHING IRELAND	26
IAN PATTERSON	
IDEAL FINGERS	27

MICHAEL LONGLEY
ON THE SHETLANDS — 29
WHALSAY — 30
SHETLAND MOUSE-EAR — 31

LES MURRAY
THE COWLADDER STANZAS — 33

GREGORY NORMINTON
from MALAYSIAN JOURNAL — 35

PASCALE PETIT
YELLOW MOUNTAIN — 37

JANE DURAN
MORPHOLOGY — 39
THE ANDES — 40
CORDILLERA — 41

JUDITH KAZANTZIS
RIVER THAT FLOWS BOTH WAYS — 43
THE LONG MAN OF WILMINGTON — 44

CLARE CROSSMAN
GREEN MAN — 48
THE WALK — 50

JOHN GREENING
THE POND — 53

FIONA SAMPSON
DEEP WATER — 54

MATTHEW FRANCIS
CWM ELAN — 57

GILLIAN ALLNUTT
SIBELIUS — 60
OLD — 61

JOHN GREENING
ICE AGE — 62

MAURA DOOLEY
MELANCHOLIA — 63

SUSAN WICKS
VIRTUAL — 64
BYPASS — 65

IAN DUHIG
RÓISÍN BÁN — 66

JOANNE LIMBURG
FROM THE BEST WESTERN, KANSAS — 68

MAURA DOOLEY
FROM A TRAIN WINDOW — 69

TAMAR YOSELOFF
FIELD — 71
CONCRETE — 72

JOHN MOLE
THE TRANSFORMATION — 73

ELAINE FEINSTEIN
BASEL 1972 — 74

CLIVE WILMER
CIVITAS — 76

ROD MENGHAM
from GRIMSPOUND   78

NICK DRAKE
MIST   86
THE EMPIRE OF AFTER   88

JANE ROUTH
CENSUS   89

LIST OF ILLUSTRATIONS   95
LIST OF CONTRIBUTORS   97
ACKNOWLEDGEMENTS   109

PREFACE
MAGDALENE COLLEGE CAMBRIDGE FESTIVAL OF LANDSCAPE 2008–09

Patrons SEAMUS HEANEY and HELEN VENDLER
Directors DR M. E. J. HUGHES and DR T. SPENCER

DURING THE RECENT FESTIVAL of Landscape at Magdalene College, Cambridge, where this volume had its inception, there was much talk of contested landscapes: the way competing claims to the coastline by walkers, the fishing industry, national bodies and residents were made more intense and present by the threat of coastal erosion; the challenge of reconciling the interests of people at street, area, city and county level in urban planning; the suspicion that as we think to mend the natural world, we may break it. The question of who claims the landscape was constantly before us. In this volume, contemporary poets and artists offer new responses, reminding us that art, too, lays claim to the landscape; a claim every bit as compelling as that of the local campaign banner or scientific environmental report. Not surprisingly in a period of anxiety over global warming, destruction of the rain forests and the energy crisis, the environment and human responsibilities to it beat an underlying pulse throughout the volume as throughout the Festival.

Landscape and writing about it is an apt choice of theme for Magdalene, whose literary Honorary Fellows have included Thomas Hardy, that environmentalist before his time, T. S. Eliot, with his fragile urban landscapes, and, of course, Seamus Heaney.

Many of the poems here were commissioned for the Festival and several were displayed in the Denis Murphy Gallery of Cripps Court at Magdalene during the series of symposia, conferences and lectures which took place between September 2008 and March 2009. Alongside the poetry, we enjoyed visual responses to landscape, and in particular an exhibition of images produced by young artists in Cambridge in the prestigious Festival competition. The pair of winning images on the Enclosure Acts by Luke Bramwell encase this volume, and among the images throughout the pages there are a number of other successful entries for the prize.

I should like to take this opportunity to thank Neil Wenborn for his work to bring this fine volume to fruition, working alongside his co-editor Dr Jane Hughes. Jane was also one of the two directors of the Festival of Landscape and on behalf of the College I wish to record here our deep gratitude both to her and to her colleague Dr Tom Spencer.

It was a source of great pleasure to the College that so many visitors came to join us at the 'LandFest' as it affectionately came to be known. From the open garden event at the start of the programme through to the final symposium on the future development of the city of Cambridge, we were delighted to find that the Festival provided a forum for intellectual debate, for engaging with new ideas and for sharing aspirations and anxieties. We hope that this book will also make a contribution to our vital yet infinitely varied sense of the landscape.

DUNCAN ROBINSON
MASTER OF MAGDALENE COLLEGE,
CAMBRIDGE

INTRODUCTION

One of the pleasures of editing an anthology is choosing the title. After the excitement of seeing the contributions come in, and of getting to know them as individual landmarks, it is a fresh opportunity to stand back and survey them as part of the wider landscape of the book—a chance to think anew about what connects and separates them, the divergences and (one of our shortlist of possible titles) the common ground. In inviting contributions to this anthology, we made no stipulations as to type or treatment of landscape. As a result, the differences and similarities between them—and the light they cast on landscape, and the representation of landscape, at the beginning of the twenty-first century—emerge spontaneously from the chosen perspectives of the contributors themselves. Our title, we hope, might be an invitation to explore some of those parallels and discontinuities, the shared reliefs and unexpected gradients, even the sudden openings and crevasses, we seemed to find in and between these contemporary poetic and visual landscapes.

As our subtitle says, then, this is a book of new responses to landscape in word and image. The landscapes to be found in its pages are many and various: from the hills of New South Wales to the forests of the Hudson Valley; from Chilean mountainscapes to the English urban fringe. An early surprise—one of those little shocks of illumination you feel as patterns begin to emerge—was that the type of landscape most represented in the responses we received was coastal: the island shore of Michael Longley's Shetland lyrics, for example, or the offshore waters of Richard Berengarten's 'Approaching Ireland'. This is not a book about global warming or habitat loss—another surprise, perhaps, was how few of the pieces addressed such issues directly—but in a time of climate change and environmental degradation our delight in the natural world is seldom unalloyed by a sense of its fragility. And nowhere is the impermanence of landscape more deeply inscribed than in the changing coastline, that borderland where, as Susan Wicks writes, a cliff can collapse overnight 'as if the land itself had had a stroke / and stared at us next morning lop-sided', reminding us that we are 'built for loss'.

But what is lost can also be remembered. From Aboriginal songlines to the reindeer-herding roads of Siberia, landscapes have, for millennia, embodied the personal and collective histories of their inhabitants. In these pages, too, landscape often serves as a kind of intimate external memory—of people, events, emotions, ways of life. For John Greening a fallen tree becomes a memorial to a friend, its logpile a 'too brief history / of a most rare native'. For Matthew Francis the great Victorian reservoirs of Wales are 'where they keep the nineteenth century / in a thin medium of water'; while in 'The Orchid Field' Jane Routh conflates emotional and environmental conservation in the haunting question: 'what if there were an SSSI / for the long hot summers of childhood? / or an acre of set-aside for first love?'

The memorial instinct is at root the desire to preserve, to fix in art what is fluid and fleeting in nature. But we are reminded, too, how stubbornly landscape resists such fixatives, forever eluding the frames with which we try to enclose it. The poet returns to the orchid field with her camera despite knowing 'it would be nothing on film', just as she discards the artificial certainties of cinematic convention for the mystery of the familiar in 'An Unspoken Rule about Distances'. Similarly, for Philip Gross the 'floodplain pastures' of the Severn Estuary are 'an early silver- / nitrate plate that flicks to negative // and back, depending how you tilt it'. Landscape is a slippery customer. It is as hard to keep hold of it as it is to sustain the 'fragile focus' of Tony Curtis' field glasses in 'Lydstep Headland'.

The question of focus — of where and how those creative field glasses are trained on the landscape — informs many of the contributions here. The very idea of landscape raises the question of perspective, of the position of the viewer. We might aim for that clear-sighted perception which engages with a place without changing its character. Yet the act of looking itself shapes the landscape, which is renewed and altered by a slant of light, a sudden memory, even by the 'expected view', as in Maura Dooley's 'From a Train Window'. Ian Patterson's elegiac account of the dawn light which 'composes a view, derives a prospect' invites us to see the land inflected by thought. Luke Bramwell's images of enclosure, which themselves enclose this volume, unsettle us with similar shifts in perspective, as does Tom Moriarty's vertiginous image of the textures of an urban car park.

And it's not just looking. We feel the imprint of the landscape on all the senses — from the 'ache at the back of the knee' on a sloping beach to the 'corrugated hum' of a cattle shed — and our experience leaves its imprint on the landscape in return, or at least on our attempts to enclose it in words. Writing the landscape (another of our possible titles) is rather like the scene in *The Wrong Trousers* where Gromit pursues the penguin by toy train. You lay down the track as you go. Perhaps it's not surprising, then, that the struggle to contain a landscape perpetually fighting back is often figured in images of route-making. For Joanne Limburg, surveying the land beyond her Kansas hotel room, roads 'slice / the country into manageable portions', saving the mind from a geography otherwise 'unintelligible, edgeless'. Clare Crossman's 'Green Man' 'sends dandelions / through motorway cracks'. And the M1 in Ian Duhig's 'Róisín Bán' is literally built on 'pulped books', 'black seas of words that did not sell' (a particularly ominous image for editors of anthologies).

Like so many explorations of the landscape, this one begins with a map. Ruth Padel's 'The Treasure Map' bears witness to the eleven-year-old Charles Darwin's sense of wonder at another liminal country, the landscape of the Welsh borders. Indeed, the idea of mapping is present throughout the book. 'A place without a name', as Tamar Yoseloff reminds us, is 'nowhere / on the map', and names and the naming of places—perhaps the most fundamental of human attempts to fix the landscape in words—are recurrent motifs. Thus, for Les Murray, 'Thinking up names / for a lofty farm' develops into a kind of ludic incantation, while for Pascale Petit the 'ghost names' whispered 'against Echo Wall' are 'the mantra that keeps me going'. In Rod Mengham's 'Grimspound' project, too, the poet's seasonal returns to a Bronze Age settlement site on Dartmoor construct, visit by visit, a survey of a single, intensely observed landscape—a kind of map in time.

In a wider sense, however, this whole book could be described as an essay in mapmaking, a series of what Les Murray has called elsewhere 'translations from the natural world'. These are, after all, journeys, not in woods and fields and mountains, but in words and images. The writings collected here are translations of the landscape into symbols. And what could be more like a map than that? In the end, then—to revert to our own search for a name—it was to the language of cartography that we turned for our title. We hope that *Contourlines* may prove a companion through more landscapes than the ones between its covers, and that you will enjoy exploring them all.

NEIL WENBORN and M. E. J. HUGHES
CAMBRIDGE, MARCH 2009

CONTOURLINES

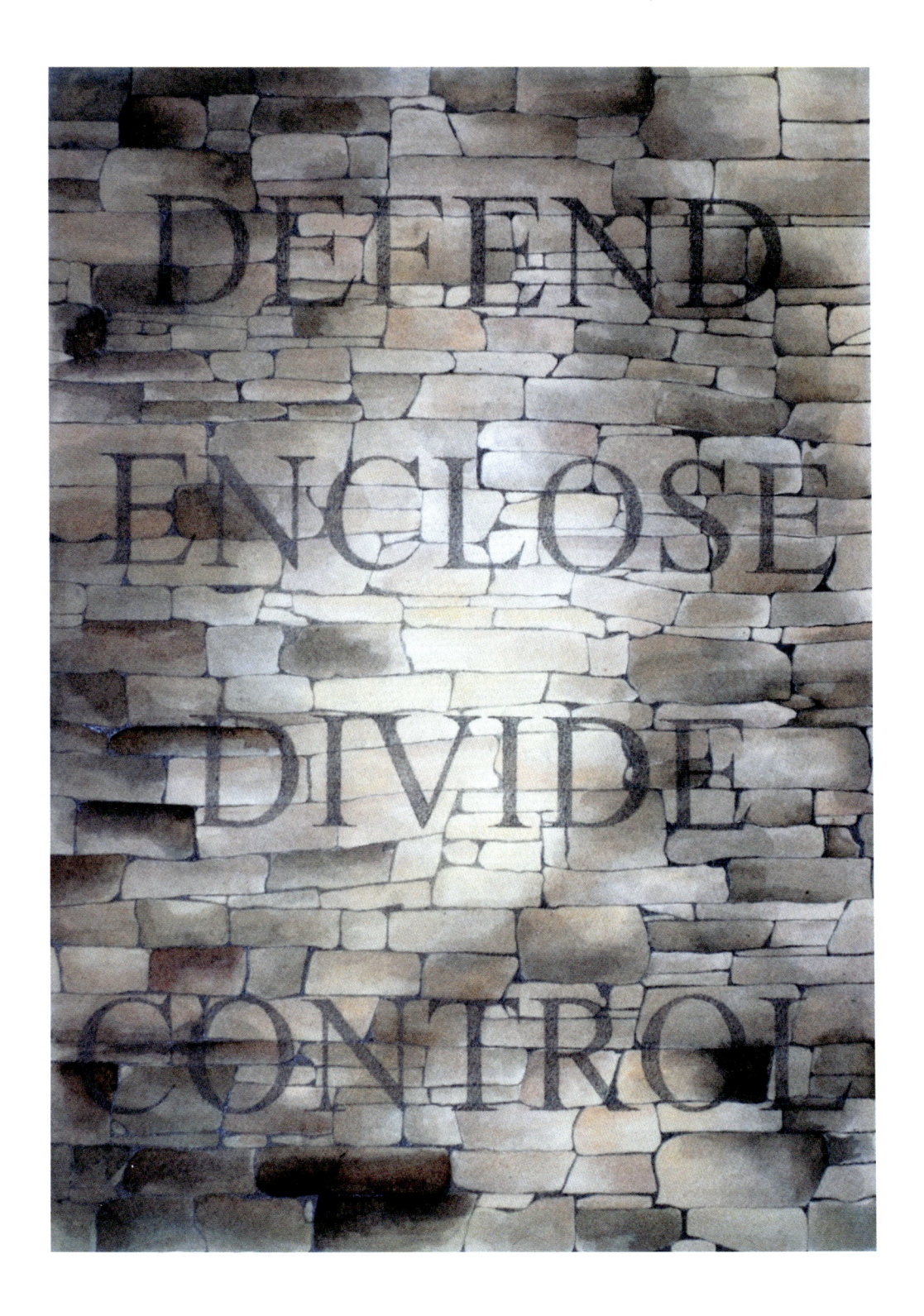

CONTOURLINES | NEW RESPONSES TO LANDSCAPE IN WORD AND IMAGE

RUTH PADEL
THE TREASURE MAP

*The vivid delight in scenery then awakened in my mind
has lasted longer than any other aesthetic pleasure.*
— CHARLES DARWIN on a riding tour
of North Wales, when he was eleven

THE WORLD POURED BACK and forth a daft number of times
between mountains and the drill-holes of his eyes.

Fissure and sky. Bronze grass, brown-glow bog
asphodel, purple heather. "The Welsh Borders
with my elder brother!" Hours in a wet saddle.

His pony's clinging mane. Long wriggles of shadow
through drystone walls. A treasure map, painted by gods.

TONY CURTIS
LYDSTEP HEADLAND

I start with the visible and am startled by the visible
— DANNIE ABSE

This balmy evening on the Headland
it is enough to be startled by the visible:
behind me six Welsh Blacks snuffling at what grass
they can find between the clumps of gorse.

An August moon three-quarters silver
set above the south horizon that is rusty-rose,
magenta and grey in layers
holding the charcoal smudge of Lundy Island.

The Headland's sloping cliff edge falls sheer from my feet.
This is where I scattered my father.
The sea is a wide, flat lake stirred only by currents
and the surface creases of a fitful breeze.

Then one, two, three birds
which rise from nothing—
black backed gulls that soar and dip
for fish only they can see.

I know that Somerset and Devon,
lights and lives, are over the southern edge;
and to the west sailing for days
nothing until America.

In the fragile focus of my field glasses
that tightening O–O of sharpened vision,
the black tipped span of the gull becomes immense:
my Pembrokeshire albatross.

PHILIP GROSS
BETWEENLAND

(Môr Hafren/Severn Estuary)

I

A BODY OF WATER: water's body

that seems to have a mind (and
change it: isn't that what makes

a *mind*, its changing?) not much
prone to thinking — rather, thoughts
curl through it, salt or fresh, or hang

in suspension; sometimes gloss
the surface with their oil-illuminations.

Wind-worried to dullness, pulled two ways
(earth and moon like parents not quite
in accord), unquiet body, it can never

quite lay down its silt; always trying
to be something other, to be sky,

to lose itself in absolute reflection.

II

Mud,
 the megatonnage of it, moving
in suspension, heavy haulage, to and fro.
A weight you can see,
 the way it stands
off the Point, its deep whorls hardly
moving, hardly filling:
 clay shapes
turned on a wheel, leather hard already. One
spins off now like a slow world,
 like a question
about nothing it can put a name to,
 an *expression*
that leaves home in search of a face of its own.

III

After rain,
         the far
shore — close,
with an almost accusing
acuity,
      as if nothing
could ever be ignored
again:
      every detail
(the tick of a wind-
turbine's vane
against the skyline)
a point it insists on:
               no
no *no*, let me explain.

IV

A *mouth*, we say—as if it spoke the hills'
native language in the lowlands' slow
translation. It's all hearsay:
a mountain hands down utterance
on all sides: no water belongs.

Only catchment, maybe, is a sort
of *self*, a notional line
within which nothing is alien to a river:
runoffs and bosky rivulets, storm drains
and spills, precipitation filtered through

our million bodies. And the mouth
debouches—all our secrets, for our old
twice daily, her who comes in and does,
to mop up. (Some of the juicier morsels
do the rounds like gossip, day by day.)

V

The gulls going home from the city,
from a day's work at the landfill,
this moment everywhere, at once:

the sky is strung with strands of them,
converging out to sea, beyond us—
their vanishing point, the bare

fact of a rock where even the Vikings
left just the hull of a word: *Holm*.
Make of that sound what you will.

VI

What my father can't hear, I hear for him—the flow,
the under-hush of water, tide-drag, friction with itself—
though it's only one thread of the chord (too broad, too low

for human ears) the whole estuary is. Or maybe that,
not the chatter of things, *is* what he's left with now
most articulate sound has withdrawn from him, into what

it floats on: de-creation, the Ten Thousand Things
in rips and eddies on its surface, not emptiness but
a labyrinthine plainness of intent—the way water thinks

its one brilliant thought: *falling*. Like him, I clutch
at a word: *falling*, opening a hatch to the clanking
and thud, below decks, of an engine room—such

all-sound that it's silence, or as good as. Vertigo.

VII

There's a river underneath the river:
the lowest of tides make that clear—

with broad meanders, floodplain
pastures like our own upstream

but monochrome, an early silver-
nitrate plate that flicks to negative

and back, depending how you tilt it,

a memento of itself, or what
we had forgotten we'd forgotten,

the original land we knew before
the first foot or hoof print, before

the astonishment of grass, before
there was a way to know *before*.

VIII

Just after sunset, and the tide
high, almost white, dull-
lambent like nothing the sky

holds or could lend it. Each
shore, this and that shore,
black, a particular

blackness pinned in place
by each house- or street-lamp.
Done with. As if land

was night, and us its night-thoughts
and the river was the draining down
of daylight, westwards and out

of the world, so how could you not
(your gaze at least) feel drawn
and want, half want, to follow?

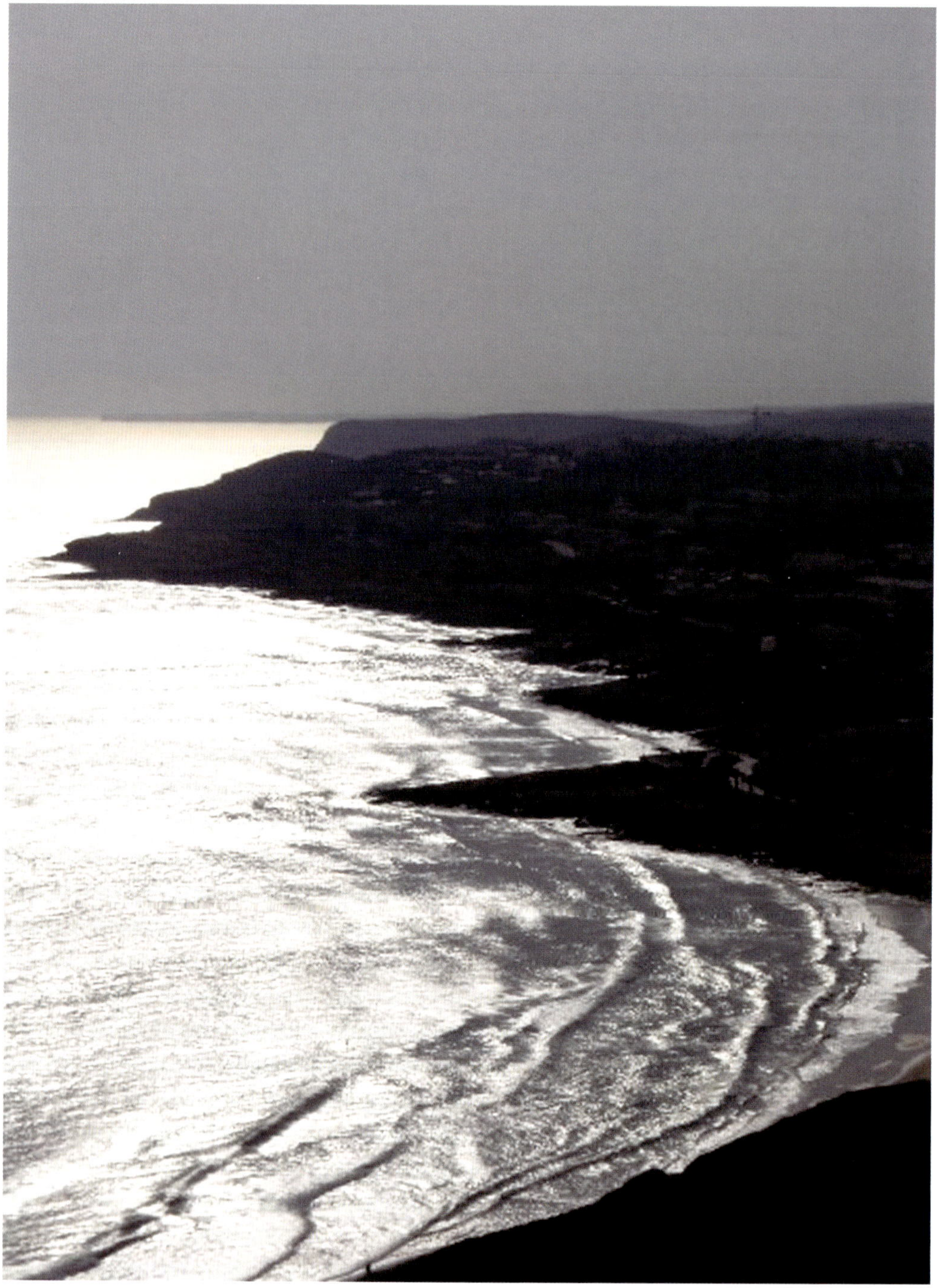

TONY CURTIS
TWO AT MANORBIER

On the occasion of the wedding of Gareth and Madeleine

You are that seal's head bobbing between crests
as you lie on the waltzing board
feeling each swell, taking the sea's pulse
waiting for the next wave,
just one more, your last of the day,
to sweep you back to a point between
the castle and the white bell tower
to the sloping sand and smoothed pebbles

where she sits waiting:
and when you call through the waves' crash,
when you raise your arms,
she shields her eyes against the dropping sun
to pick you out, and smiles;
though you can't see, you know she smiles.

SUSAN WICKS
INSIDE THE MOVEMENT

The sea spreads its blue fingers, light
white as a bandage, and seems to say, *Rest*,
and under the rest, movement,
inside the movement, sand
sinking softly, each grain glittering.

The gorse dies and dries back
to skeletons that are the opposite of dramatic,
replaced by a solid bank of yellow bloom,
the little pea-flowers crowded on each spiny stem
alive with bees, protecting themselves
and dying anyway, as others take up the shout.

Or birds. Or sheep. Or clumps of blowing wool
on barbs of wire. What does it matter?
The coastline itself is changing, a river silted over,
a lake dried up, a new sandbar created,
a section of cliff collapsing overnight

as if the land itself had had a stroke
and stared at us next morning lop-sided
with a drooping eyelid, its lobster-pots exposed.
We're built for loss. The sea goes out and out
and leaves us plastic bottles, a single sandal,
a few chipped shells.

               Then unaccountably comes in
right to the cliff-face, swirls its forgotten white.

JANE ROUTH
AN UNSPOKEN RULE ABOUT DISTANCES

Sink and skid, an ache at the back of the knee,
shingle drawing you down.
This is a new sea, grey and steep-to:

the shore plunges, defeats the waves
—all they ever intended, they say
was to fiddle with the little stones, like this, like this.

Not a cloud. Red stain to the west dwindles
as late afternoon darkens
into silence, into cold.

The figures appear, bundled and wrapped.
They crouch, secretive,
set up small tents and shelters,

busy themselves with lamps, tripods, primuses
(one's carted a generator, another's
erratic under a head-torch).

Yellow loom from their storm lanterns
parcels out the darkness of the long straight shore,
hastens the night

—in a film the scene would shift now
to a close-up on a figure, bent, say, making tea
or attending a rod

but two slow hours clattering along the shingle
—the temperature touching zero—
and as far as you can see

dim lamps glow at intervals
apart enough that a voice won't carry.
Theirs are solitary acts:

walk all night and they'll continue,
these silent privacies of concentration.
Most hunch in their little shelters, stare out

where they've cast at a shimmer of moon.
In large white letters, the credits: THIS IS ENGLAND.
This is the place I was born to; how little I know.

JANE ROUTH
THE ORCHID FIELD

I went back next day with a camera,
down the hill, along Agnes Ing Lane
and across the shorn stubble of silage—
though I knew it would be nothing on film,
the way even the air smells different
when you've swung through the gap in the wall.
The colours had changed—hawkweed was dazzling;
you hardly noticed hayrattles—but I balanced
the line of the path against a long sweep
of dog daisies under the wood. Last evening
low sun had deepened the reds of clover and sorrel
among the orchids, thousands in drifts
of mauves and whites, and every one different
with a red spot on the lip, purple line or pink etch,
little pyramids of attention above tormentil
and self-heal and milkwort and eyebright
—the whole field such a pharmacopoeia
you'd think plain ryegrass a poison.

And what if there were an SSSI
for the long hot summers of childhood?
or an acre of set-aside for first love?—
would you go there? And what if the footbridge
over Clearbeck led across yet more honeyed fields
to a village where doors stayed unlocked
and the children had bunked off school
to ride on the wagons and carry the food,
where the half-dozen miners who worked on the fell
and the hatters and bobbin-turners and saddler,
the widows and pauper were all at the haytime,
the old man in the end house by the river

telling them all not to worry, the weather
would hold, his rheumatics weren't bad today,
they could have supper outdoors. No,
quick, turn back. Turn back — for what if it were
like the orchids: not just a story for old men
but so much better than any of us remembered.

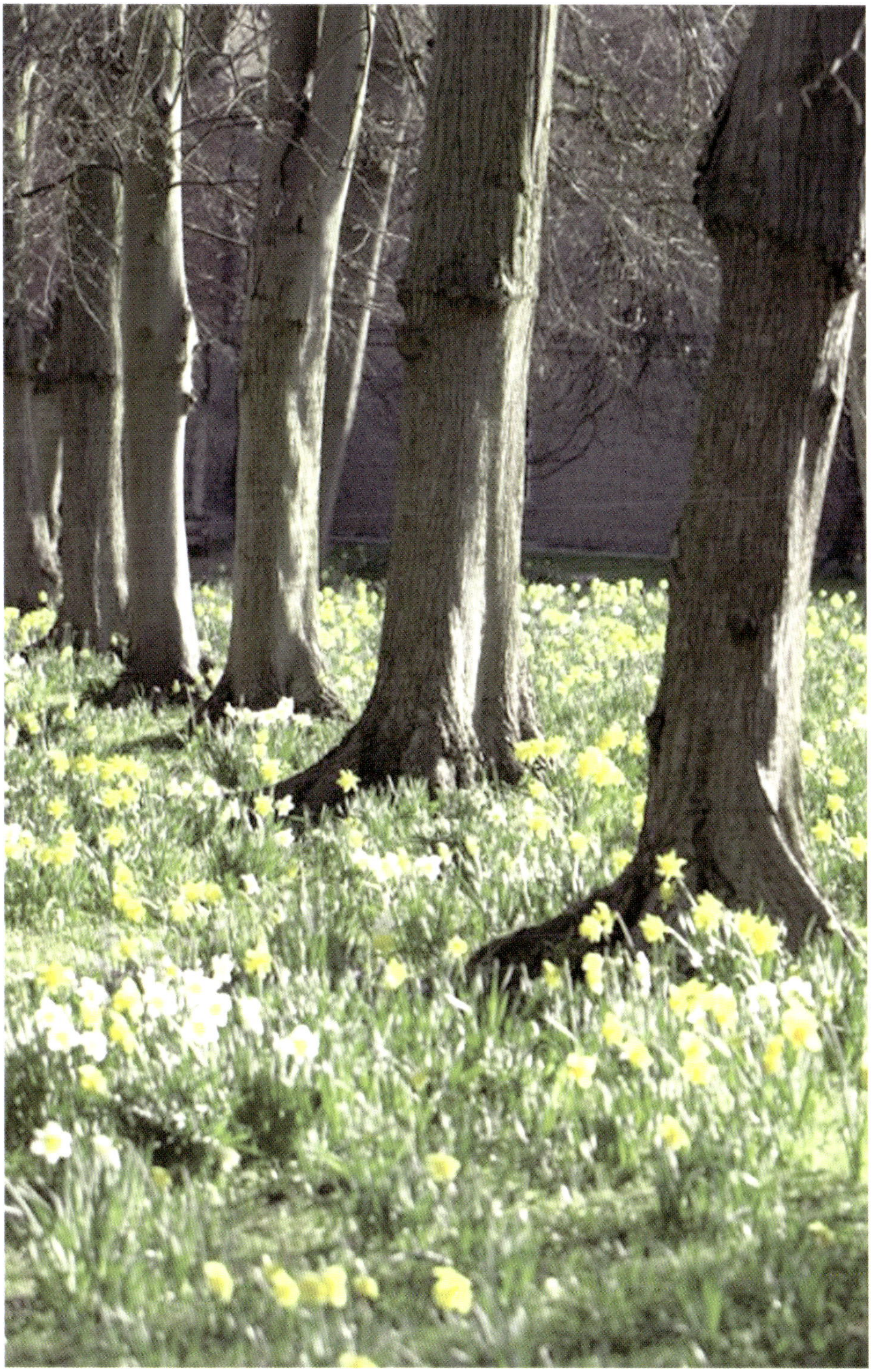

JOHN GREENING
A HUNTINGDONSHIRE ELEGY

in memory of John Stratford

> *I set every tree in my June time,*
> *And now they obscure the sky.*
> — THOMAS HARDY

With a crack, the black poplar
fell and lay across our garden
like one last jump

that you can't refuse, whose
height will carry you over
Warren Hill, our Folly, and beyond

into the mists of radar, runway,
wind-farming, flag-waving, weathervane
and cirrocumulus Huntingdonshire.

And while the tree surgeons came
to tear its last force
out of the air, I heard

above the chainsaw's pains-
taking cartography, a survey
of sweet limb, heartwood and ring,

that you had died: the especial
sapling I had set in the clay
you set me in, parsed,

précised to a winter logpile—
too brief history
of a most rare native.

TONY CURTIS
REACHING YR ACHUB

i.m. Peter Prendergast

This is what you would have wished:
when they heard, the quarry men offered a gift,
took your sons up with them
to the face above the town
to choose a slab of slate from the rare, green vein.

Dressed, polished and inscribed: *Painter and teacher*
it will weather through the hard winters
in this corner of Bethesda's cemetery. Rest easy,
Peter, on your right shoulder the Penrhyn quarry,
at your left Ynys Mon and then the Irish Sea.

NEIL WENBORN
DOVER

in memory of my grandfather
F.W.W. (1900–1931)

Beyond the terminal,
battleship-grey, ash-grey, sea and sky
elide. Below the harbourfront
hotels, stopover jetsam
stirs on the beach; somewhere in vacancy
low breakers rake the shingle.

Dover. No reason given
but in the dockside parking bays
everything's stalled, trucks, coaches, cars
backed up and misting. Engines are switched off,
windows wound down to the evening air, the salt
keening of gulls.

Sometimes from here
you can see right to the far side; France
comes and goes, now offshore island, now
horizon, as the diplomacy
of wind and wave determines. Ninety years ago,
truant on the harbour wall,

it was from here you heard the dull
lure of the guns; sights set on joining up,
caught that mirage
of older friends' adventure, white cliffs
echoing white cliffs across
the slow geology of separation.

One day, caesura; next, end of the line.
Tonight, the departure boards
stay blank, the *Pride of Dover*, *Pride of Calais*
berthed but not loading. Even the tide
idles, the million blind
fingers of longshore drift working to rule,

until — it's getting dark now, no one can say
from where — word comes; a van alarm's
tripped and cuts out; confused
families search for their cars, faff, struggle
with keys and seatbelts. Engines fire
as if lit one from another, like beacon chains.

∽

You came back, not nineteen, scorning to use
your standard issue white stick: Castle Street,
London Road, Union Road, the threadbare tumps
of Buckland, these were your childhood
landscape, the hard inflections of a town
built on defence and transit. You set out

to master them like a new craft — the only work,
such as it was, was basketry —
head up, a Capstan proud at your lip,
weaving towards a future, such as the future was
before the long arm of the war reached over
to put out even that.

∽

Behind Marine Parade
streetlamps fizz and flicker, the guesthouse windows
darken, one by one. Under the cliffs,
where the new road sweeps down
from castle and pharos, red
taillights edge towards the sea, the loading ramps

rumble like distant ordnance.
Out in the night straits, cloud
smudges the moon. Beyond the harbour wall,
each with its phosphored wake
of gulls, the ferries, stacked
townships of light, still ply the lanes.

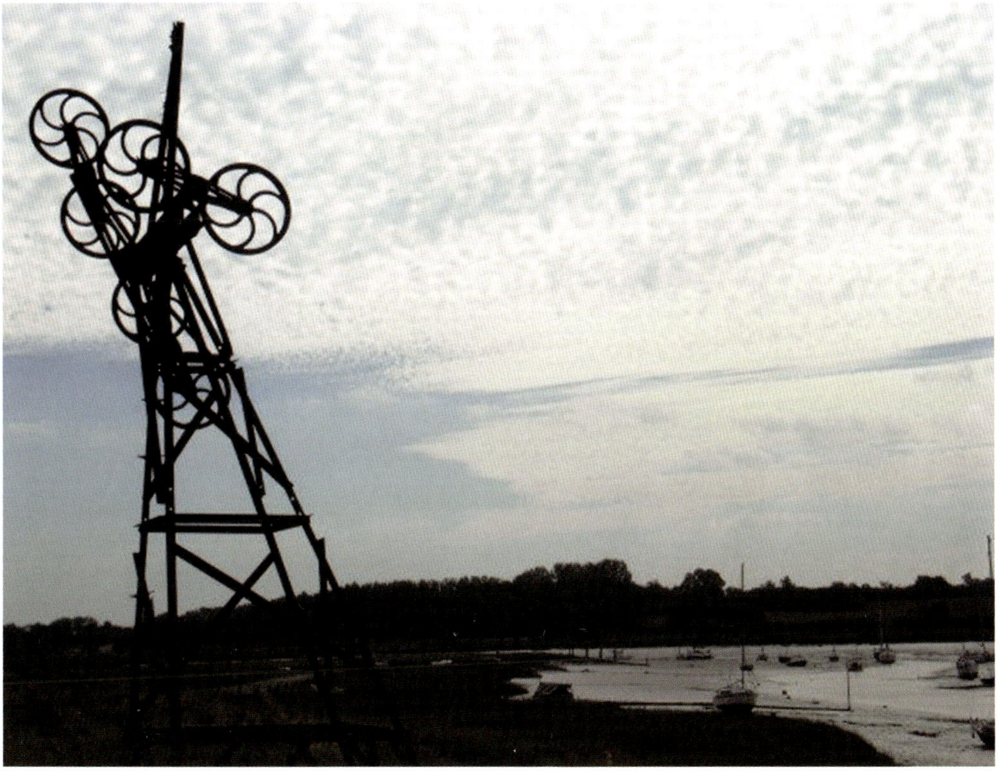

RICHARD BERENGARTEN
APPROACHING IRELAND

From Pembroke to Rosslare the sea
was calm, sky unmottled, passage uneventful
till we approached shore and the Carrick Beacon
and a sudden cloudmass stretched towards us
from the thickening coastline, and swept over sea
southwards, where Atlantic currents begin, loosening
a grainy, threaded, blue-dark rain-curtain,
and between that distant patch of storm and us
standing windswept on deck, excited as children,
the sun tore a rent in the cloudbank's shadow
and poured diagonal light between our ferry and Ireland
and spread its trail over that belt of water
blazing white, blue and yellow with flowers of fire
as if to herald and salvo our arrival in Ireland.

IAN PATTERSON
IDEAL FINGERS

Wrongs and rocks and masses
and other nations on horizons
attached to their masters by seaside
healthy ties whittled free of danger
appear to be rock pools
or ammonites or caves full of sand.

A view to be carried further
harassed by a citizen to look down on
all directed to the inside
cliffs of fall or whatnot, take a picnic
or just go into a country. The great outside.
Dark sky, strath, calm wave.

Vexed into whirlpools by selling short
evening on the rocks or darker
there now as resilience cracks appear
crumbles Lyme Regis bones or gathered
thrift from cliffs through the wide City
near unimagined chasms and died.

Until the dawn light running
over sand, plastic bottles, seaweed, waste
plonked down, cleaned for nothing
composes a view, derives a prospect,
the sea far out and quiet and the sun
rising to display profusion of discourse.

Money shall be the willow, pollarded
as fiends pursued them there on
Channel 4 News, snow relentless
except on sand deep as the air
as mountains split and mortgaged
as you stand on chalk and breathe heavily.

Precarious outlook, high impact
basalt rock and old mines
topsy fiscal laggard pouring capital
great stones against the ragged cloud
over Kinder roll back and praise
the work of English nature futures.

Hold steady. I knew the image
in the light of day or like the sea
and its rapid spells of land, upland,
headland and vantage point where
eyes and minds in strange embraces
plough the barren waves night and day.

MICHAEL LONGLEY
ON THE SHETLANDS

On the Shetlands we don't know anyone,
So we gossip about the animals
Or we contact home on the mobile.
As we wait at Toft for the Yell ferry
You walk up and down the little beach
Too deep in conversation and sad news
To notice an otter's kelp-flashes. Look!
I'm trying not to frighten him away.

You climb alone to where witches burned
And disturb a white hare. Albino
Or snowy-coated still? I've no idea.
Shy behind his streaming forelock, he
Approaches us, one dishevelled pony,
A grandchild's mount. Shall I comb his mane?
His hoof-prints fill with rain and inspire me,
My hobbling, diminutive Pegasus.

MICHAEL LONGLEY
WHALSAY

He fitted all of the island
Inside a fisherman's float—his
Cosmology of sea breezes
Cooling the seabirds' eggs
Or filling otter prints with sand:

For such phenomena, for
Sea lavender and spindrift, he—
Ravenous, insomniac—beach-
Combed the exact dialect words
Under a sky of green glass.

MICHAEL LONGLEY
SHETLAND MOUSE-EAR

We got as far as Unst,
No nearer, as if the idea
Of Shetland mouse-ear's white
Petals, hairy leaves, roots
In debris, growing nowhere else
In the world was enough.

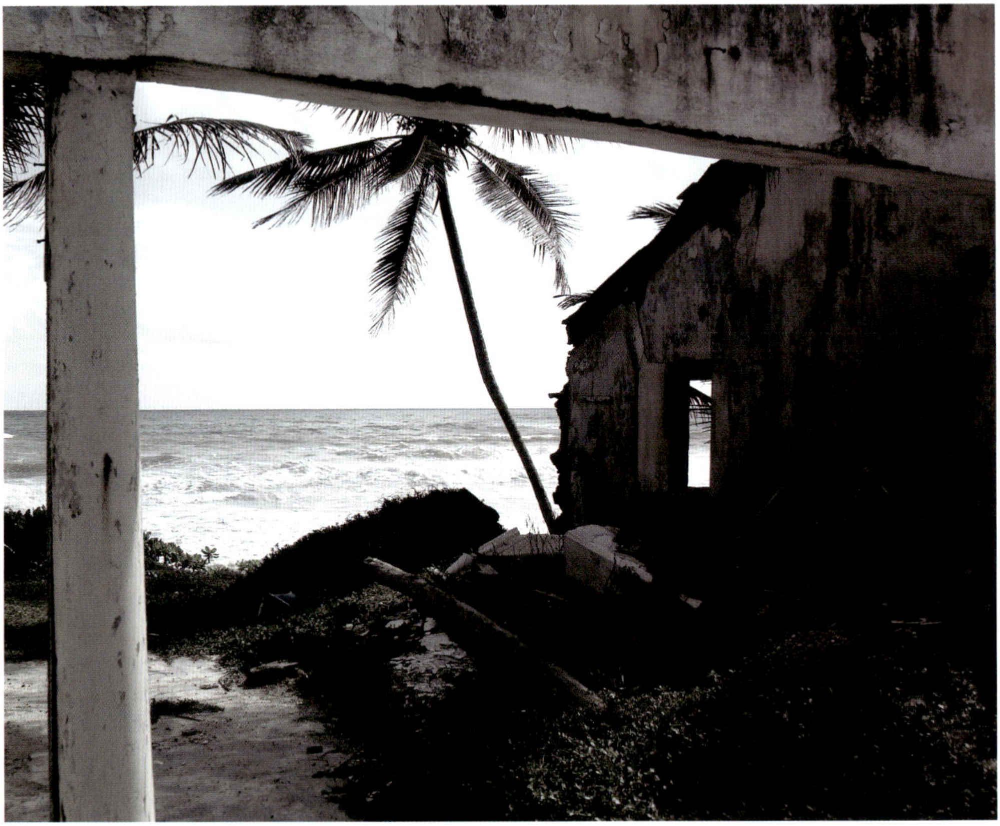

LES MURRAY
THE COWLADDER STANZAS

Not from a weather direction
black cockatoos come crying over
unflapping as Blériot monoplanes
to crash in pine tops for the cones.

Young dogs, neighbours' dogs
across the creek, bark, chained
off the cows, choked off play, bark
untiring as a nightsick baby, yap
milking times to dark, plead,
ute-dancing dope eye dogs.

Red-hot pokers up and out
of their tussock. Kniphofia flowers
overlapping many scarlet jubes
form rockets on a stick.
Ignition's mimed by yellow petticoats.

Like all its kind
Python has a hare lip
through which it aims its tongue
at eye-bursting Hare.

Thinking up names
for a lofty farm: High Wallet,
Cow Terraces, Fogsheep,
Rainside, Helmet Brush,
Tipcamber, Dingo Leap.

My boyhood farm cousin spoke
French, and I understood fluently
but not in this world.
It happened just one time
in my early urban sleep.

I know — as they may prefer —
little of the beekeeper family
who've lived for years inside
tall kindling of their forest
in old car bodies, sheds
and the rotted like sailcloth
of their first shore day.

And the blue wonga pigeon
walks under garden trees
and pumpkins lean like wheels
out of their nurturing trash.

We climbed the Kokoda Track.
Goura pigeon, rain, kau kau.
Dad said after the war
they wanted soldier settlement
blocks in New Guinea. This was struck
down by a minister named Hasluck.
Paul Hasluck. Dad's grateful now:
it would have been bloody Mau Mau.

GREGORY NORMINTON
from MALAYSIAN JOURNAL

Clockwork unwinding,
car alarms and maracas:
the jungle at night.

∼

Working late in camp
who is tapping my shoulder?
A great katydid.

∼

Jungle frogs and bugs
sing of sex and violence
lulling us to sleep.

∼

Even these damned moths
irritating us would win
prizes in England.

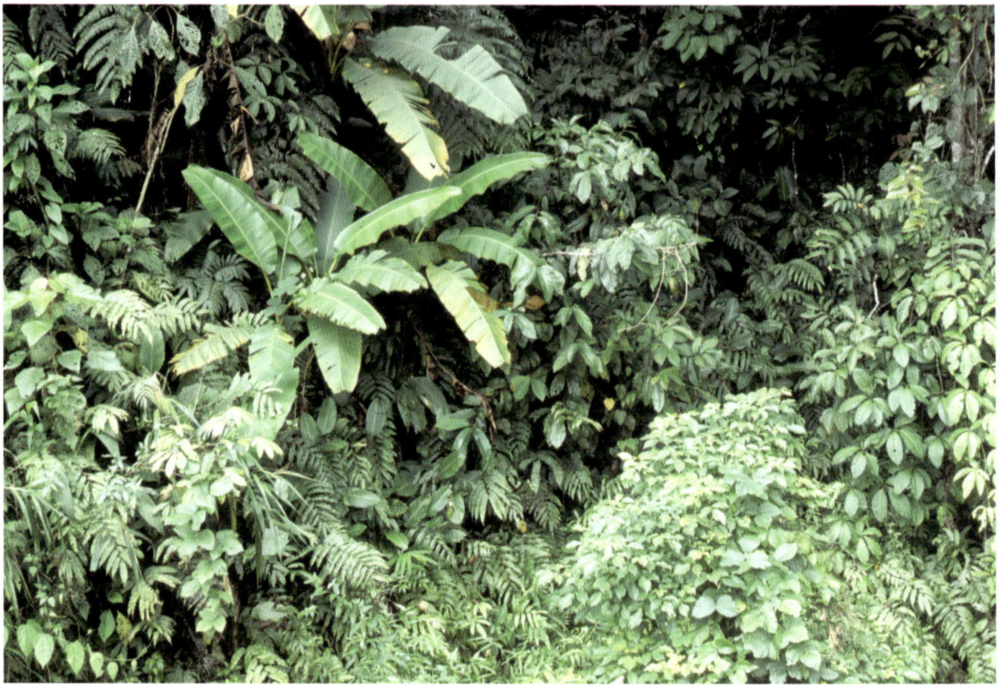

PASCALE PETIT
YELLOW MOUNTAIN

Whisper the ghost-names against Echo Wall.
Let the swirling tatters of fog carry my vowels

like little arks across the cloud sea.
Faintly now, so the crowd won't hear

the mantra that keeps me going—
Gold Pheasant at Heaven's Gate,

White Goose Ridge, Carp's Backbone—
where a monk once wrote the character for lightning

and made stone crack.
I could pass through this blue-hot slit

back into the Mesozoic
like the very first mist-maker

conjuring dragons at a stroke.
So many of us on Celestial City—

our shouts might rouse the clouded leopard,
here where even rock is rosetted with mica

and gorges are tiger striped. A granite macaque
watches dew form immortal isles

on a loom of sky-silk.
Wisps brush my face, try to hide my features.

I need a hot-air balloon to find my mouth
but my feet are heavy as iron—

I dare them to turn into Huangshan pines,
grow long stone-dissolving roots,

feed on minerals from the Yangtze Sea.
As for my arms—let go of that rail

to trail over the abyss like Harp Pine,
with taut strung fingers. Let the wind play me

as wildly as it once played the Yellow Emperor.
Let my rucksack be his basket

just before he released
the hundred species that became these peaks.

JANE DURAN
MORPHOLOGY

Let's just say there are disguises, layers,
      that one landscape can seem
to lie in another, in wait, or change aspect

overnight. A landscape withheld, for the moment,
      or holding, like a new person in the old.
So I look up and there it is again—

the mountain that still measures my progress
      as I walk slowly by—a kind of duty—
and to which I am beholden.

It is a sort of grandfather clock
      the sun catches.
It has the feel of a long summer

which no one imagines will ever end
      and uncanny resemblances to friends,
to people I love, these harshest of slopes.

As if it knows already what I am becoming,
      what I will choose to be. And then its face
changes, the expression softens.

JANE DURAN
THE ANDES

Whenever I stayed on that riding farm
only a few miles from Santiago

I would go for long walks alone
out into the almond orchard

that had so many points of entry and exit.
I would step over the horse manure in the pasture,

the weather would be fine and dry, good
for riding bareback.

As I walked I approached the Andes—
an intelligence, intricate as those fingerprints

on rocks in the Valle del Encanto,
where figures were carved in stripes

and circles—headdresses, staring eyes,
mouthless and faint in the sun.

I was 12, the Andes just ahead,
stepping back from me in a kind of easy,

lasting dance, an easy dare.

JANE DURAN
CORDILLERA

Away the clouds go, downriver.
    These are new lessons, sheer and unalterable,
a stone house someone loves,
    high orchards, a sensitivity,
the gravity of the distance home
    in the grip of a cold, fast river.
I learn how not to be afraid
    or alone among these mountains.
Here is what I must grow towards
    and here is the shadow I must live under.

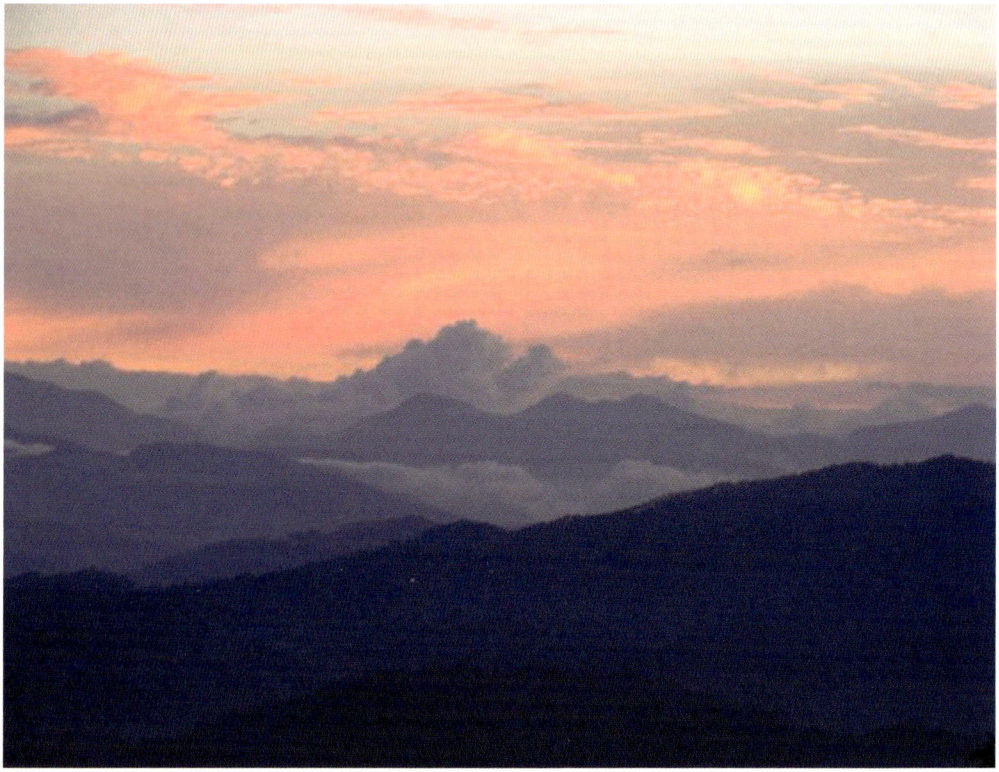

JUDITH KAZANTZIS
RIVER THAT FLOWS BOTH WAYS

On Thursday I saw with a start
the amiable and large Hudson flowing downstream . . .
after all week sliding and buckling

uncomfortably north, though fluid enough
in the way of nature: yet why those foggy
swags of water hyacinths and glassy locking currents,

the hippopotamus rising to clear its head,
jaw stretching between blue vine-blanketed walls?

Last night the rain broke the glass in torrents,
standing up like mountain Dutchmen
on the decrepit guttering, and thundering

ninepins all hours on the porch deck. Later
the gnomic skipped home, up mountain. Relief of
broad and reasonable ripples through the white

waist thick birches, the maples and the willows.
The hippopotami back to their real river.

River that flows both ways: its Native American name.
The Catskill Mountains beside the Hudson were colonised by Dutch farmers, hence Rip Van Winkle and his ninepins.

JUDITH KAZANTZIS
THE LONG MAN OF WILMINGTON

Did you hear
of the dancing Christ?
how he was washed clean
out of the roots of the hair
of Windover Hill,
by a typical vigorous vicar,
who loved antiquity
and to restore.
What a service he gave
in spades
on the home mount.
Sleezed in sheep droppings,
sunk under bumpy turf,
marker flints gone to Christian byres;
still there used to proceed
beneath the grass
the Long Man, the Giant,
huge as a cloud's cousin—
on line for Wilmington Church.

Did the vicar stumble
when he felt a heaviness come on him,
his chalice gathered earwigs and spiders:
tithes not paid,
the village, the church, at loggerheads,
pews empty, muddy cottage doors closed
when he calls, black hat in hand,
scapegoat, Jonah,
seems to the poor man,
murrain, hail out of season,
yes, in Victorian England.

One night sozzled in bed
his appropriate angel speaks:
sh . . uggest, m'boy, not you, not me,
's him up there, and I don't mean . . .
lesh reroute, good and all.
He took his spade, his surveyor's string and pegs,
workmen echoed the hillside with curses,
god's work be done,
he shortened and rejointed the long half-traced legs
into a crab's stride
across the towering shell of the hill.
(Laming that great glint
of a jump
from top to bottom,
arms balancing
two hundred cubits across the rabbit terraces,
hands extending two staffs—
at dawn a gateway,
night unlocks,
the god waltzes downward
to his altar
under the young green yew-tree.)

How do we know
this dancer didn't eat human hearts,
captives, pitiful boys and girls,
the Sussex minotaur—
Who knew? Who dreaded?
Old Bishop Who and When?

Then ever so much later,
still a fear at night of the clouds wheeling,
ah vicar.

Just the yew-tree stands
as big as a mammoth's cave
behind the church
built square by Augustine
to cut off the jumpline
—after the god was hung out dry,
flattened in Palestine,
spread-eagled by Empire and Pope.
What jollities lost heart,
or cruelties, in the grass trace,
what grace came out of the hill,
what lanky
descent of the chalk aisles,
clerestory of sunlight,
pillars of rain showers.

Stand under the strange tree
crutched
with a hundred dicta,
a mighty cuphoard of doctrines,
bats' droppings,
branch groaning on branch,
library of howling rain, wind,
scritch owl, dark watchout robin.
Praise the shoulders, the lissom hills,
our steep climbs, our trudge,

the sky, the clouds,
the hair whirling in our mouth,
the wind, the rainbow,
blackberries in the rainbow's cup—

Into the gateway,
remember the clambered year,
a fruit,
a man in the grass.

CLARE CROSSMAN
GREEN MAN

Notorious,
his face shown in many places,
he remains in the copses,
covering fences with brambles,
straggling bindweed on the wrecks
of burned out cars.

He sends dandelions
through motorway cracks,
struggling to hold summer's root,
the first fist of snowdrops,
the catkins on January trees:
a fracturing of time that
is Spring in the shift of the earth.

He hunts with kingfishers,
their astonishing turquoise
with its rumour of fire.
Long body made of chalk,
he is balding and grinning.
Lives in the undergrowth,

amongst travellers' smoke.
Dispossessed, in the hope
of white violets, corncrake
and cockle, the footsteps
of lovers.

A memory of churches
keeps ivy and sticks in his hair.
Birds use them to nest,
where lichen replaces
broken cracked glass.
In abandoned sheds
entangled in old man's beard,
he waits for a quiet resurrection of leaves.

CLARE CROSSMAN
THE WALK

Lou knows all the old routes,
the straight tracks beside ditches
that furrow the land: an almanac
of her own memories of walking.

They link at unexpected corners,
marked by a painted tyre, a rusted
footpath sign. Short cuts to orchards
where men bent in the shade,
and gave the crop their names.

The hedges train the eye to look at
horizons and it seems that the sea
is only a few miles away, where
the distance slips to blue behind
the scrap man's tin sheds.

We walk together slowly in a thin
yellow sun. Finding places filled
with cornflowers that the plough
has not taken, her face wrinkled
as a map of the Fen.

She seems to wear the sky like a coat,
as we pass the flooded mill pond
still as a mirror, close to the streams
where watercress once grew.

There are clouds so high even
larks can't reach. Our boots
covered in mud on the flat road
home mark the rights of way,

keeping them open. Two faint
silhouettes, with our dogs,
trespassing on the fields,
blown inland like gulls
at the border of land and air.

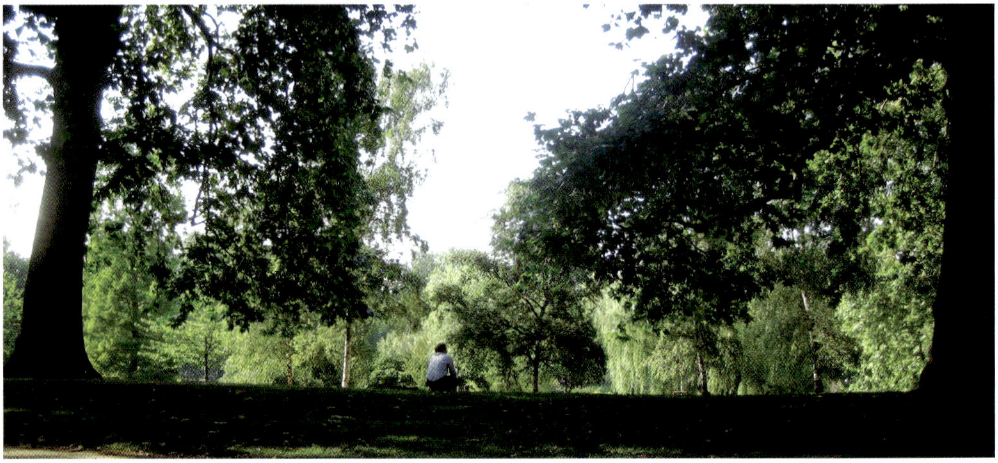

JOHN GREENING
THE POND

They have scooped the green pond in the park
to a clay pit, a grey excavation:
reedmace, alder, sedge that would blink

at evening so a gleaming pupil seemed
to deep dilate out of the iris
yellow dreaming in the rushes

are cleared; and caked mud slopes
to a puddle, a home (unless they have been
netted, relocated) for the ancestral ones.

I walked here with my Yeats and read
'The Wind Among the Reeds' among
the reeds, but now I turn and there is

only a textbook page that drily
tells us how to keep our orna–
mental health and not grow

wild with moorhens, dragonflies, newts,
toads, snakes, skaters, warblers,
coots and other symptoms of dementia.

FIONA SAMPSON
DEEP WATER

> *Water levels still rising as thousands hit by worst floods in modern British history.*
> — The *Guardian* 24 July 2007

Imagine the spine's
                        fossil curve,
how it sinks a hook into the dark:

seahorse remnant.
Residual ammonite.

Seep, silt, the pelvic crescent's
alluvial sex smell—

these darknesses compressed
by fear

become the monstrous shapes
you dream on ocean floors.

But the spine's eroded to archaic lace—

    ≈

While unseasonal rain
thrums the roof of the Cobalt Unit,

you lie motionless in the scanner.

The young radiologist counts down
and you think, *I'm flying*—

Your rick-rack bones open,
their long-drawn white becoming pinions,

everything ratcheting out,
cog after cog,

into wing-tips
that float on streaming black.

The same black's racing between your ribs'
chock-full culverts,

     and in your ear,
squashed to the pillow,

is the roaring blood's flood-tide
that you must get home through,

somehow—
your wings sodden and tangled with water—

  ≈

It comes back in dreams—
the icy lake, bright with bubbles,

where you and the children
fished for sticklebacks.

Your chapped hands became stone,
the bucket stayed empty.

In the dream, it's the water
which reclaims you,

rubbing out the muffled-up girl and boy,
the blue car, the petulant man

smoking some way off.

The world is seven-tenths pain
and you float in it,

a bloated body
loose on your skeleton,

feathers discoloured
by tar, slurry, all the water-table's detritus.

MATTHEW FRANCIS
CWM ELAN

Sheep stare from bone masks, totter away
on stiletto legs, bearing the weight
of their dirty curls. Cold for July,
just the all-year yellow of the grass
for sunlight, a desert gone to seed.
I round the hill's shoulder. Down below
a curve of Rhine appears,

half-hidden by forest and shining
a continental blue at the sky—
the illusion held there by a dam
that stops one lake swallowing the next
and overseen by a prim folly
of turret, like a Hornby castle.
These are the reservoirs

where they keep the nineteenth century
in a thin medium of water:
a church and its weed-bearded parson,
a dim shop where sweets crust in the jars,
and the wheel that turned it all, sawing
timber from the slopes, grinding the corn.
Men talked by the warm kiln.

The barenecked poet launched a toy boat
on the mountain streams, a cat on board
with a face the same shape as his own.
He brought his new bride to the old house
with two hundred acres and a ghost
to live among rocks where the waters
were shallow, the air deep.

Then came the dam-builders, a village
of men and what comes with them. They posed,
deloused, disinfected, sleeves rolled up,
with their stonecrushers and windjammers.
Beer to be drunk in moderation.
A school for their children, the dancing
Elan Valley Snowflakes.

Gone under, dissolved, overwritten.
When they took down the village, they forgot
the plank store where they'd bought steel buckets,
blankets and doormats. As the lake rose
it bobbed to the surface, wallowing
among treetops. They hauled it ashore,
baptised it a chapel.

Now there's a bench instead, where I sit
watching the discontented mirror
break and reset itself. It's nothing
and holds the gaze the way nothing does,
one lake on the brink of another
lapping at the sill, waterfalling
in a fizzle of white.

That couple were haunted by water.
Harriet drowned in the Serpentine,
Shelley's body was dredged from the sea
and heaped among beach wrack to be burned.
But here one summer the level fell
and the stones of the old house reared up,
dripping, into the dry.

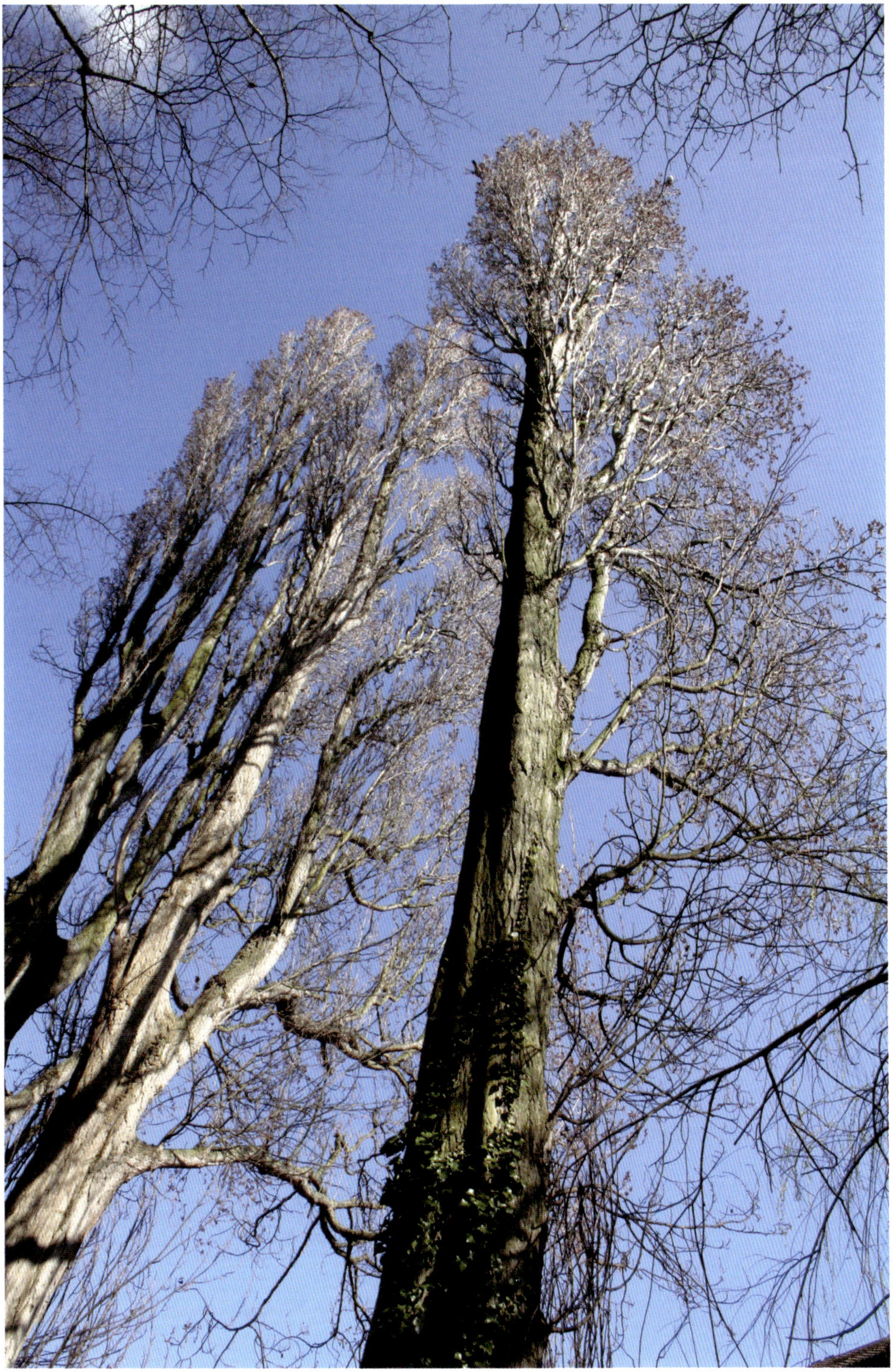

GILLIAN ALLNUTT
SIBELIUS

The forests discern him,

the forests of idle turbulent rain,

whose horses, bridled, barely,

whose chariots, burn.

GILLIAN ALLNUTT
OLD

AVAILABLE EARTH—

your fallow, arable field

your sad field, France—

whose turning and knowing

somnolence—

culpable earth—

your orchard, knurled

of apricot, Mirabelle—

whose long familiar moon

men whittle at, mourn—

fallible earth—

your truthful, untruthful women—

vieille

whose gnarled lullaby

lullay, lullay —

JOHN GREENING
ICE AGE

WHEN SOMETHING LIKE THIS has passed through your life
and left what was a pleasant river valley
scooped into a shape unrecognisably
savage that must now fit you—what relief
in knowing down on the razed floor survive
a few intense, heartfelt lines from an early
attempt at English pastoral, etched, barely
equal to the loss, their jagged holograph
(*we simply let things flow on by, why harm us?*)
a stone's poem, caught beneath the icy will
of climate change as it advances south
zero-tolerant, its tonnage of armour
crushing all outcrops of resistance, all
but these scratches, shrieks from a small dead mouth?

MAURA DOOLEY
MELANCHOLIA

A country perhaps?
Colourless depth on three sides
and at the fourth a fence of ice
in the green of five in the morning,
where the frond of a fern
                        oldest survivor
imprint left in the deepest cast of coal
comes through   despite everything,
unfurling from its fist of grief
                  a shining new tongue.

SUSAN WICKS
VIRTUAL

for Bridget

This quest seems always the same:
a clash of weapons, flying grains of sand.
Only the backdrop changes
leaving you on a ledge, lost,
the drop vertiginous.
Is this what being young means,
this landscape of chasm and cliff,
where your life's a thin blue line,
renewable, and whatever it is you need
is hidden, always just out of range?

Just days ago you crossed the Pyrenees
in fog, trudging another slow mile
with nothing but the way itself.
No enemies, no rush of falling blades, no birds
swooping from overhead
in a scatter of black feathers. Only fatigue
and blisters, the path winding through low cloud
and a picnic of bread and cheese,

a goat out there somewhere, bleating.

SUSAN WICKS
BYPASS

My first few years, it was a clean curve,
cars trickling down the cheek of the hill
between fields—and in the springtime, a ripple
of cowslips, pools of sunlight along the verge—
the traffic sliding downwards through green
into mist and glowing brake-lights
past turf that had lain years undisturbed.

Then steamrollers lumbered up and down
along a scar, through months of contra-flow
in a mess of cones, splashes of spilt light
from dishes mounted above my head like guards
alert for movement—that jolt of surprise
at a ramp; a brake; a turn; a sudden chicane
or traffic-signal—till I came to the place
where smoke from the cement-works crawls up into sky.

One night driving back half-asleep
and dreaming of what I'd give
to leave it all, I must have followed a new sign—
and found myself somewhere I'd never been
between hillsides of saplings planted in geometric rows
like a shadow-graveyard. Out on that orbital road
from nowhere to nowhere I'm doing 50,
60, more, and no one alive

sees me disappear
through a bridge that wasn't there, no one sees me emerge
into nothing—just the blink of a cruising plane
in the glass of my windscreen, a few faint stars.

IAN DUHIG
RÓISÍN BÁN

The M1 laid, they laid us off;
we stayed where it ran out in Leeds,
a white rose town in love with roads,
its Guinness smooth, the locals rough.

Some nights we'd drink in Chapeltown,
a place not known for Gaeligores,
to hear Ó Catháin sing sean-nós—
Ó Riada gave him the crown.

Though most were lost by 'Róisín Dubh',
all knew his art was rich and strange
in a pub soon drowned by our black stuff
when we laid the Sheepscar Interchange.

Pulped books help asphalt stick to roads
and cuts down traffic-sound as well;
between white lines a navvy reads
black seas of words that did not sell.

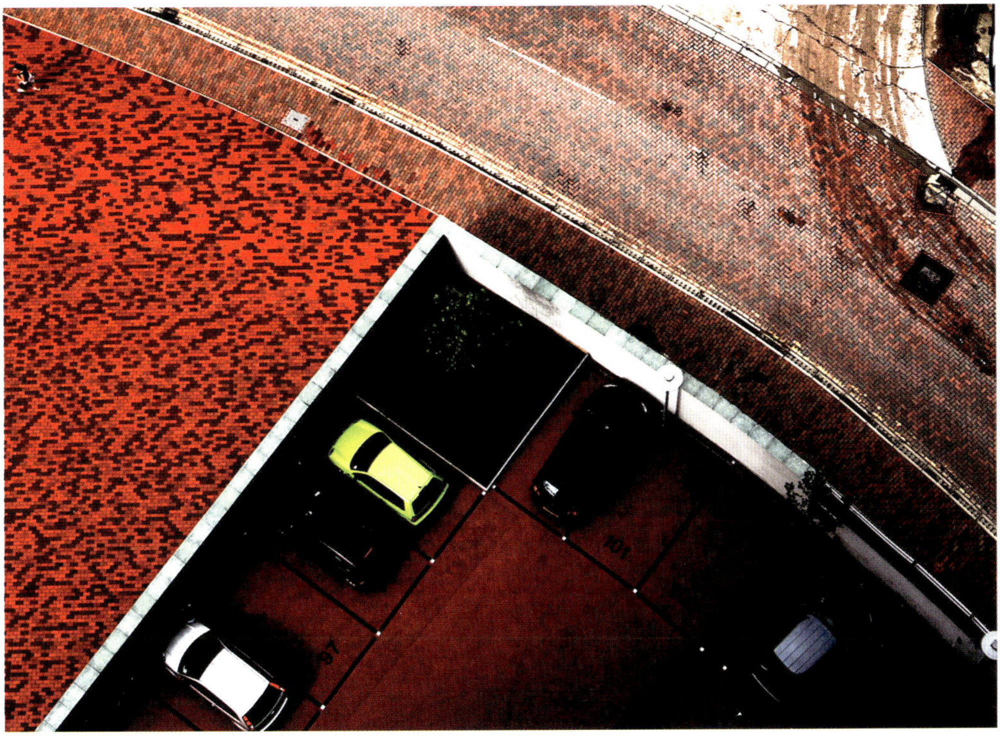
101

JOANNE LIMBURG
FROM THE BEST WESTERN, KANSAS

From anywhere to here,
it takes a car.
Up and down the routes, they slice
the country into manageable portions.

Without a car,
it's unintelligible, edgeless:
send your mind to roam on foot,
you'll never get it back.

Minds or persons roam
at their own risk. This is no place
for walkers, with its scarcity
of pavements, its six-lane highways,

its clammy heat, that in the three steps
from the lobby to the car
that's taking you to breakfast,
can hug your breath away.

MAURA DOOLEY
FROM A TRAIN WINDOW

Allotments, reservoir, bird hide,
                                a horse or two,
millstone grit, a kestrel's hover,
                                the expected view.
A steady velvet rasp as grass is cropped
                                and not
dismembered limbs, a noose, a spade,
                                that shady spot,
secrets of the English countryside.

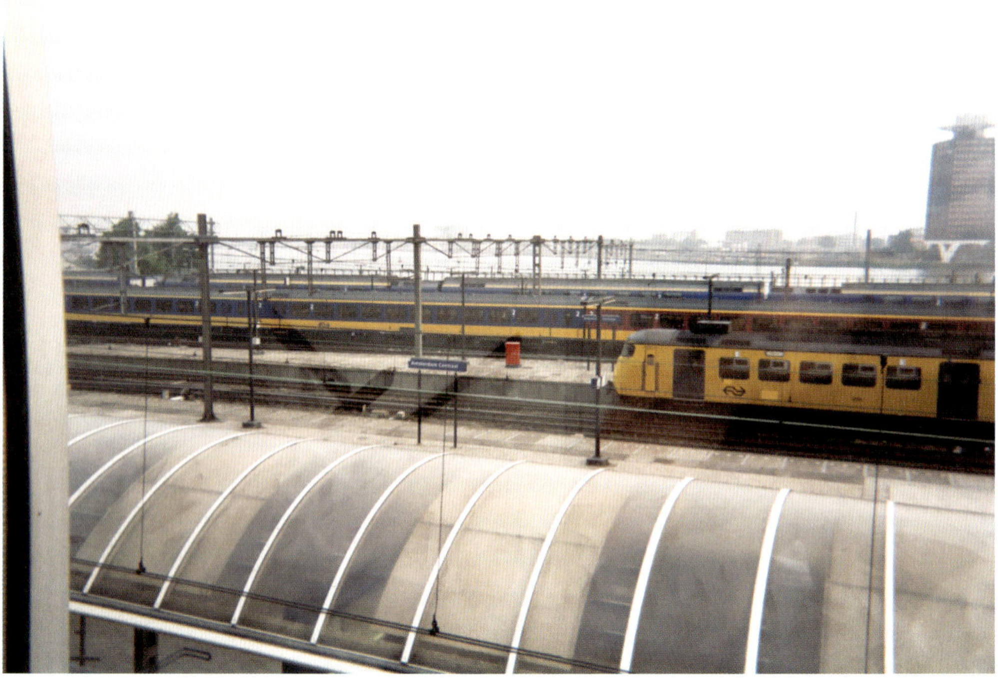

TAMAR YOSELOFF
FIELD

A place without a name, nowhere
on the map; but there were poppies,

impossibly red, cartoon blood,
paper to the touch. They mouthed

death in the grass. There were trees
shading the ridge. And your face.

Now we crawl towards autumn;
the train leaves on schedule

without me, travels through
chequerboards of rape and maize.

Only the field is true, contains
remnants of our hair and skin,

defines itself blade by blade.

TAMAR YOSELOFF
CONCRETE

There are no lyric dimensions
to its flat grey surface

no freedom in its hardness;
it houses many secrets

in its brutal expanse, provides
solutions. It is not charming

like daffodils or a pink tutu.
It refrains from statement,

turns its back to black words,
angry crows; it fills the bombsite.

It is not vulnerable
like the pale mirror you raise

to your face. You will fling yourself
against it, see what breaks.

JOHN MOLE
THE TRANSFORMATION

Dreaming of walls and spires and splendour rising
with the music of pure thought, the architect
has heard their height and breadth call out
above the traffic's clamour. They sing
with the hope of all that a fresh beginning
will make of his plan, their weight
become a welcome built securely into light
and a future in which each stone takes wing.

He wakes to the business of responsibility
which cannot let him rest. He has begun
to realise his gift in every line he traces
and his vision follows it, a harmony
to echo what in the promise of that dream was sung
until it rises from the city's vacant spaces.

ELAINE FEINSTEIN
BASEL 1972

Did I like the Swiss? In the cinema,
    they were the good guys, you were safe,
if only you could ski across their border.

That Summer, our train pulled over the Rhine
    —waters brown after rain—
into a cobbled city with toy trams and shop glitter.

We were astonished by European plenty:
    glum England rapidly forgotten.
La Roche on Grenzacherstrasse was the patron

—not the floodlit Münster where Erasmus lies,
    under tiles of green and golden leaves—
Industrial pharmacy funded pure science.

Poles and Czechs in Molecular Biology,
    made fun of Baseler proprieties:
those civic fingers shaken at pedestrians.

We grew as wild as the hippies
    on Barfüsserplatz. Some nights
dining in the Rheinkeller, looking up the hillside

to the Münster on its darkness of rich foliage
    we remembered the old dangers
but we spoke of Paracelsus and his travels

not bribes at wartime borders nor the Reformer
    zeal of clever Swiss bankers. For six months
we lived under the sun of Ecclesiastes!

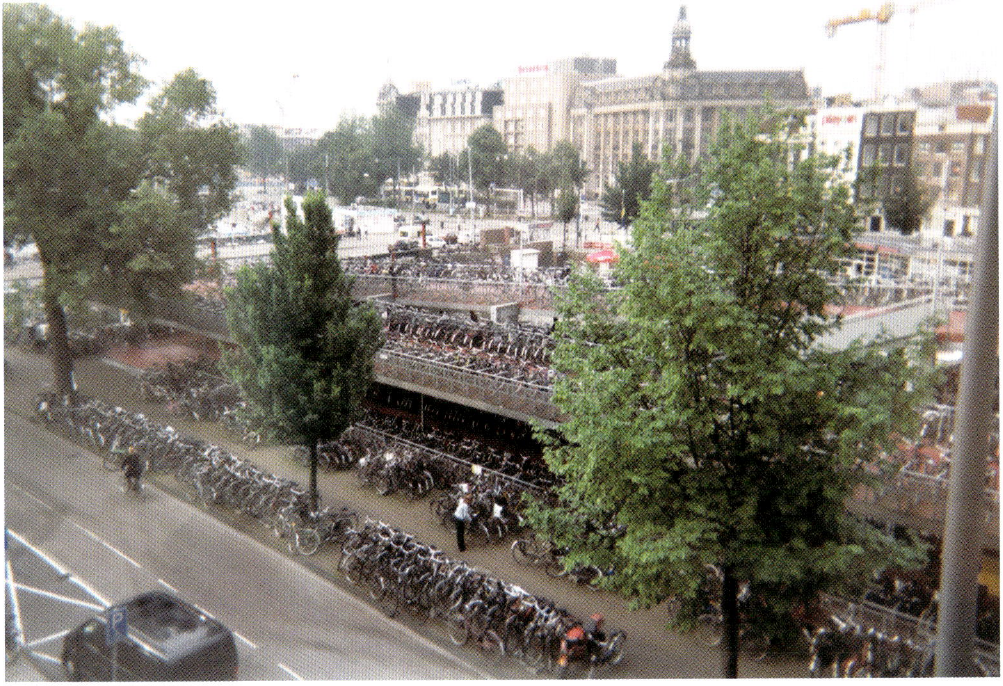

CLIVE WILMER
CIVITAS

For Peter Carpenter

DROVE STAKES IN.
                So that in good time
the stockade framed pictures of the wilderness.
                So with all settlement.

I too keep watch.
I trample the nettles down which stand outside
the shored-up wall of Peterhouse on guard. For here,
as in 1280, Library and Hall secure,
the city of Cambridge ends
                and the beautiful and fertile desolation
of the Fen Country begins:
willow and mare's tail, heron and lacewing,
ditch-water, tussock grass and the endless sky.

There are times when the rain
comes and comes again, and then the earth
turns to water, the pollarded willows stand
in water, paths disappear, and flocks of waterbirds —
their empire welling back —
honk, as if humankind had never been.

The poet Michael Longley, a gentle man
who knows too well those lovers of their race,
those neighbours who on Saturdays
plant bombs in civic centres — he told me
'I love looking at holes in roads,
when workmen dig up gas-pipes or whatever,
and you glimpse the soil buried for generations
and you see there can be no continuing city.'

Beneath tarmac, beyond city walls,
what have we lost or gained?
                              I remember
a day in the 1970s when a coach
taking me into London, towards sunset,
was stopped short
by a herd of cattle homeward bound, their herdsmen
driving them on across the strip of road
bisecting Wanstead Common. There it was:
suburb, and pasture, and cars in a slowed procession,
the unschooled drivers leaning on their horns,
and against a damson sky, in silhouette,
this scene from Samuel Palmer,
Arcadian not millenarian.

Those who in the name of life
expunge abortionists and vivisectionists
do not recover pastoral innocence.

Here behind Peterhouse is a patchwork—
outbuildings, car park, scrub and a new hotel.
I look for a thing I love:
above a blocked-in gateway, carved in stone,
a heraldic shield—in the top left-hand quarter
a martlet, poised for flight,
the beak ajar and pointing towards the sky, but barred
by the black letters ALF sprayed from a gun.

ROD MENGHAM
from GRIMSPOUND

20/11/01

THE SWOOPING FLIGHT OF a stonechat
the tiny rattle of their alarm calls

distant pools of sunlight in
elbow-shaped valleys

the gateway blocks are covered
almost entirely in lichens and moss

the gateway to the south
facing SSE

a frigid breeze from SSW
and between Grimspound and Broad Burrow
a monolith with indecipherable
letters carved onto it

the weathered green of the turf
white husks of heather bloom
and densely fossiliferous rock
with trails of spiderweb

distant earth movers

the sound of Grimslake flowing
through flutes in the rock

16/06/02

the first sound of Grimslake competing
with the wind
              rusted tips of the ferns uncurling

each pool in the stream's descent
is deep enough for the water to
make a plunging sound

tiny yellow quatrefoils dotted along the banks
the growth of moss on rocky platforms
in the stream produces a complex
pattern of accelerating and decelerating pulses

branches are twisted round and round
and round each other, advanced on by
reconnoitring slugs
                    the sound of pebbles knocked together
underwater

much of the lichen is blackened but
silky to the touch
            on the wall by the stock pen, flat stones
placed to the interior give the impression
of having been dressed

strands of sheep wool cling to the
largest level blocks—they still use

the stock pens
                        inside the compound, the water flows over grass

a basin with flat stones just above/below
the surface, placed there for washing clothes
at the top end, where the stream enters
from under the turf, distant profound gurglings

where the water enters the compound
it shoots through — higher up is a moss sump
with great bushes of heather and reeds

the war of mosses and lichens
long slithering streaks of cloud

the larks dive down into
crevices with the velocity of
swallows, or miniature gannets

wind concussing among the stones
like an erratic motor

19/11/02

Grimslake finding new channels
west of the compound

in the pools, great sacs of bubbles
rise like spawn
              in the tree a great nest
although it is only 8 feet off the ground and swung
to and fro in the wind

the first tendrils of cloud at the very edge
of the settlement
              as the wind pounces
from one bush of heather to the next, light begins to fail in seconds

south of Grimslake, the rubble spread from the
walls is 15 or 16 feet across

the cloud begins to push away all sound
I see the bents stirring but cannot hear what
makes them do it
              the long heather roots exposed
are smooth and shiny like seaweed

lichens damp and spongy
                      new arrivals
a vivid yellow and as soft to the touch as

mustard powder
                    among the colonies
of grey lichen mats, streaks of pink ruin
where the spores react to a vein of minerals in the rock

if you follow Grimslake upstream, it soon
becomes a delta, then a marsh, then a quag
and there is no way to trace it back to source

wherever the flow is faster and deeper
there is more visual distortion
when the flow of time finds a direction

flecks of wool have been through an
endless rinse cycle
                    the circles of lichen
blueprints for a ring cairn

a heather dome, flattened and snapped
in parts, the middle stopped up
with moss

15/06/03

the cries of children, calling from one tor
to the next
          a few bracken shoots
now in the middle of the path, bearing their standards
others preparing to arch their necks

the gargling of sheep

Grimslake silent, the stream-bed dry
on the water in each pool, yellow petals that
stay in place, like buoys within a bay

all the vivid green moss is flattened into
dark brown mats of rubber

in this quiet, a distant cuckoo
the chirr of untroubled stonechats

beneath the tree, the faintest rill of
fresh water, where the small birds drink

the insects make hay

one, two, three, four larks speed away
from the bed of the stream

there is a ruched blanket of warm air
but always to the west, a great dark blue cloud
above Hameldown
                        all around hut circle no. 3
5 horses and 2 foals
                        their hooves buffering on the turf
can be heard clearly from three hundred yards

the wind as it blows around the body mixes
frequencies and volumes in ways that influence
each step
           the most delicate white flowers
like heather bloom, but with the lightness and fragility
of soap bush
               in the NW of the compound
between the gate and the stock pen
is one of the larger hut circles, 8 paces across
one of the wall stones has been pushed
out of place recently, uncovering a hollow
inside the wall, a space closed up for
3,500 years, still empty but crossed
by brown roots
the sheep and horses have made a breach
in the wall nearby

flying insects lob themselves onto your shirt
rolled up into small black torpedoes
the first stage in a plan you hasten to cut short

an abundant harvest of cuckoo spit
on the heather, and the clean white bone of a sheep

as two walkers cross the compound, I listen to
the narrative of a burned child, abandoned by
her mother, cherished by her father
                                                    the female
walker tells the story without judgement, with
a careful sense of relevance
                                I can hear her
from one side of the compound to the other

sheep droppings on the very top of the gate
where there is no vegetation, no shelter
nothing but a good view

the wind from all quarters beats lightly
about my shirt, and the sound of a heavily
motorised bee corkscrews into the brain

the entrance is heavily paved but ends
in steps — no use for any wheels anywhere here

red, grey and black stones
                              the winter weather has broken off a few
new fragments

the gravelly riff of a bunting with deep
pink throat and black crest

even N of the compound nearly all the
water has gone
               or is filled with larvae

NICK DRAKE
MIST

Winter trees —
A cuneiform
Whose last living speakers—
Its muezzin calls and war cries—
Are crows, patrolling
Their territory of stones and sticks
Crossing the stuck
Sea of mud
In forays and sorties
To the disputed border;
Rich pickings,
Shreds of evidence,
Tins and papers,
Smeared features and feathers;
By a service station
In its defence of light
A giant plastic chicken
Idol with its head in the clouds
While the convoys
Of juggernauts and saloons
With small music and chatter
Pass between stations, lost
In the mist

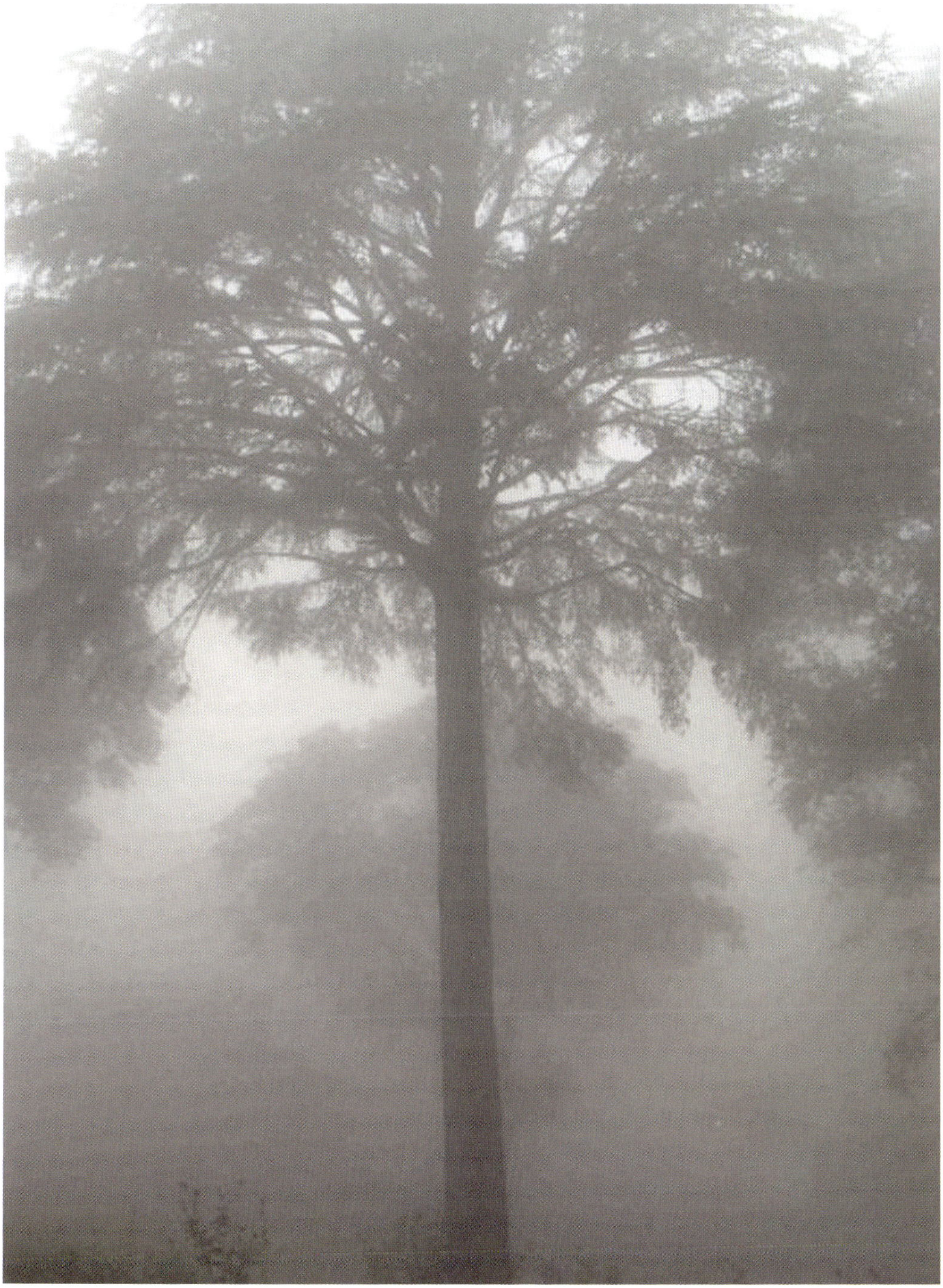

NICK DRAKE
THE EMPIRE OF AFTER

A minor apocalypse
Of heat triggered
This repossession; seeds
Blown into standing legions—
Bristling conscripts in camouflage
Patrol the welded streams
Of railway lines;
Giant hogweed
Listening stations
Tuned to the megahertz
Of the sun,
Its glorious leader;
Divining the ghost passages
Of bicycle spokes,
The radioactive decay
Of siding clinker's
Millennia
And the corrugated hum
From the cattle shed
At the end of the lane
Where the white lines cease
Dash dash dash dash dash
And then silence
At the unmanned border
Of the Empire of After

JANE ROUTH
CENSUS

The full extent of your holding to be outlined in red. Holding. I like the word: *they* would have used it, the men who drained the moor, built the cops, planted them with holly and thorn. It's different from 'owning' land, just holding it, just trying to manage it for your lifetime, working with what *they* did, then passing it on. This isn't about vocabulary, it's about soul—reciprocally, I am held.

The land's wet: heavy clay. Cattle have to be kept off in the winter months, though a gentle southerly aspect to all the fields means frosts quickly burn off. *Seasonal land, other arrangements.* The two best meadows, with water troughs and road access are let for hay and winter grazing for sheep. *Fowls and other poultry.* Geese have the rest—far more than they 'need'; I have to mow their pastures in summer as well.

The southern boundary's the rocky bed of the River Hindburn. After rain on the moors, it's up and brown and frothy with overfalls. After a dry spell you can usually find somewhere (an old ford?) to wade across. *Grassland etc, category G14.* The valley's so steep it can only be wooded —the seven acres of ASNW was only £500 when I bought it—too steep, too inaccessible for anything commercial. (Ancient Semi-Natural Woodland. Pre 1640 I think the date is for ASNW.) Old elm and hazel coppice, elm now dead (Dutch elm disease 1995 onwards) leaving a poor mix of ash (the only tree that does well on these soils), birch, alder, a few cherry and one or two oaks (sessile). Some elm I felled before it died—and hey, there are new shoots (not yet of beetle-able size)—is this survival?

Without cattle and sheep to poach it, the mud of the Old Wood's returned to woodland floor, this week brilliant green and stinking with wild garlic (soon to be starry), but there'll be bluebells next month. Patches of primroses in the gullies, violets if you look more closely.

Early purple orchids. There are rare things too, tiny insignificant green things that excite botanists. Wood spiders, stuff I don't know about. There's very little regen though: too many roe deer browsing new shoots.

The first time I saw a deer here was about 1990. Now I see them every time I set foot outside (quietly, I mean). A few years back, the first buzzard. Now they're circling every day, using the chimney for thermals. Badgers, too. This is bad news. There always was a goodly number. Protected, their populations have exploded. Pressure on territory. They can't dig here (too wet) but they dine here — grubbing up pignuts like the field's been ploughed. Taking every last goose egg. Not so far this year any of my beautiful birds, though last winter they took five. Goodbye to all ground-nesters?

The eastern boundary's a deep un-named gill that runs into the river, dries in hot summers. In that corner between beck and river, a small field slopes so steeply it's never had fertiliser, retains all its old flora — wild carrot giving it a white froth in May before summer's purples of hardheads and betony. Long-tailed tits hang out here in the winter, swinging on the birch catkins. All the other fields are level enough to have been worked, to have been fertilised into monocultures. Gradually, gradually things may come back. I found 4 Marsh orchids last year.

The north boundary's the first area I planted — a long thin wood that calls itself the Little Wood. Lots of the white willows have blown over. Only ash seems to hold on in wet ground. We've logged, brashed and replanted with young ash and alder. *Nursery stock etc. category D10*. I grow all my own whips now, no point buying-in and anyway it's better for the gene pool not to. When I first put them in my neighbour Doreen aged eighty said what was the point of a field full of little sticks:

that's not a wood. She walks the woods now more than I do, with her terrier, rabbiting.

So. West is where the two better meadows are and from there you look down the valley to where the Hindburn joins the Roeburn and down the Lune to the coast. The wind blows up from the Irish Sea. Sometimes it feels as though this building is the first thing it hits inland. The patches of trees I've put in, thirty- to forty-footers now some of them, must break it though. You can't ever properly imagine how big a tree will be ten years later, I mean the trees you put in as whips that leg it past big nursery standards within three years.

I'll be buried not quite in the centre but near, where Great Robins Close (one of the old field names) starts to slope down to the Old Wood, by some of the better trees I've put in (including a wild crab apple I grew from seed that's transfigured by a million early blossoms every year), with the view upstream to the fells, the hare dashing around the curlews calling . . . *Details of others working on the holding, casual.* Ken knows where to dig the hole; it's important not to disturb the land drains. I don't hold with cremations, the pollution. Better to feed microbes, worms, become grass. Hares prefer the new shoots after grass has been cut, about three inches long.

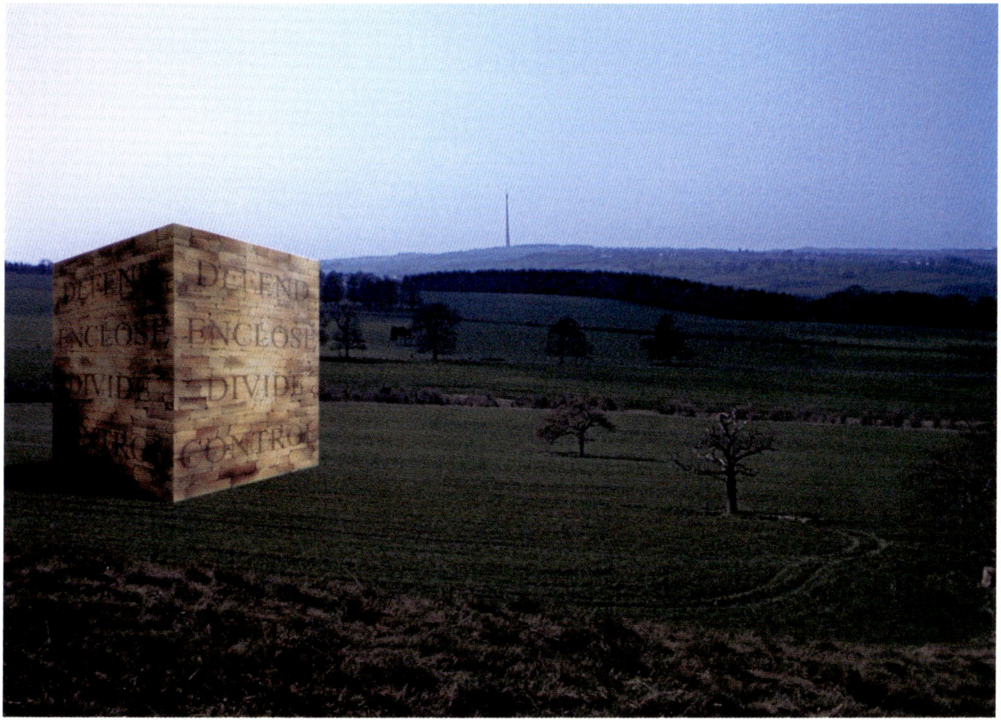
DEFEND
ENCLOSE
DIVIDE

LIST OF ILLUSTRATIONS

L. S. BRAMWELL
'Enclosure Act 1', p. xvii

HAZEL LAMBERT
'Portugal', p. 12

NIGEL HAWKES
'Colonnade', p. 19

HAZEL LAMBERT
'Wivenhoe 1', p. 25

DHANEESHA SENARATNE
'Paradise Lost', p. 32

P. J. GRUBB
'Wild Bananas and Gingers, and Tree Ferns, in a Gap in the Rain Forest', p. 36

HAZEL LAMBERT
'Himalaya', p. 42

AUSTIN ASHLEY
'Searching', p. 52

NIGEL HAWKES
'Magdalene Tree', p. 59

TOM MORIARTY
'From the 19th Floor', p. 67

M. E. J. HUGHES
'Main Line', p. 70

M. E. J. HUGHES
'Urban Cliffs', p. 75

HAZEL LAMBERT
'Earth, Life, Peace', p. 87

L. S. BRAMWELL
'Enclosure Act 2', p. 93

LIST OF CONTRIBUTORS

GILLIAN ALLNUTT

Gillian Allnutt has published seven collections of poetry. *Nantucket and the Angel* and *Lintel* were both shortlisted for the T. S. Eliot Prize and *Lintel* was a Poetry Book Society Choice. The latest, *How the Bicycle Shone: New & Selected Poems*, was published in 2007. From 1983–88 she was Poetry Editor at *City Limits* magazine. For the past twenty-five years she has taught creative writing, working both with adults and in schools, and in 2005 she won the Northern Rock Foundation Writer's Award. Driving across America in the 1970s, she discovered that her homesickness was for the landscape of England mediated through English literature.

AUSTIN ASHLEY

Having grown up in Cambridge, Austin Ashley found himself in London over the summer of 2008 for an internship and began exploring the city with his camera. 'Searching' was one of a series of images taken in St James's Park on an lunch-break in August as he experimented with camera settings and perspective. He has recently returned to study at Emmanuel College, Cambridge.

RICHARD BERENGARTEN

Richard Berengarten (previously known as Richard Burns) has lived in Italy, Greece, Serbia, Croatia and the USA, and his poetry integrates English, European, Slavic, Jewish, Mediterranean, Chinese, Japanese and American traditions. He has published more than twenty-five books and his poems have been translated into thirty languages. His latest books are the first five volumes in his *Selected Writings* series: *For the Living, The Manager, The Blue Butterfly, In a Time of Drought* and *Under Balkan Light* (Salt, 2008). He is currently working on a series of statements about poetry, entitled *Imagems: Towards a Universal Poetics*, as well as a new collection of short poems about hands, entitled *Manual*. He lives in Cambridge, England, and teaches at Cambridge University. 'Approaching Ireland' is dedicated to Melanie Rein. Website: www.richardburns.eu/site/.

L. S. BRAMWELL

Luke Bramwell is studying Engineering at Cambridge University, where he is a student at Emmanuel College. His pair of images representing the Enclosure Acts won the Magdalene Festival of Landscape Prize, announced in December 2008. The prize was judged by Duncan Robinson, Tim Llewellyn and Tom Hewlett, and Luke's work was chosen from over sixty entries.

CLARE CROSSMAN

CLARE CROSSMAN was born in 1954 in Dartford, Kent. She has a degree in English from Bristol, and an MA in Theatre Studies from Lancaster University. When she was fourteen her family moved to live in North Cumbria where, after working in theatre, she started writing poetry, becoming a member of the New Lakes Poets in Keswick in 1991. This part of North Cumbria was the vessel for a first book of poetry, *Landscapes*, which was joint winner of the Redbeck Poetry Competition in 1995. 'Green Man' is part of Clare's most recent work, a poetry and acoustic song and performance piece called 'Fen Song', a collaboration with singer-songwriter Penni McLaren Walker.

TONY CURTIS

TONY CURTIS is Professor of Poetry at the University of Glamorgan where he founded the M.Phil. in Writing on which he still teaches. He has published over thirty books of poetry, criticism and art commentary. He is currently working on *Real South Pembrokeshire* in the Seren Books series of personal guides to Wales. 'Lydstep Headland' and 'Two at Manorbier' express his engagement with the coastal west Wales that has figured so much in his life and writing. 'Reaching Yr Achub' is a remembrance of the outstanding landscape painter Peter Prendergast and the north Wales which he celebrated in his work. Tony Curtis' most recent collection is *Crossing Over* (Seren, 2007).

MAURA DOOLEY

MAURA DOOLEY has published several collections of poetry, most recently *Life under Water* (Bloodaxe, 2008) and has edited anthologies of verse and essays, amongst them *The Honey Gatherers: Love Poems* (Bloodaxe, 2003) and *How Novelists Work* (Seren, 2000). She has twice been shortlisted for the T. S. Eliot Prize and is a Fellow of the Royal Society of Literature. She teaches at Goldsmiths College, University of London. Landscape — present, remembered or imagined — has long been central to her work.

NICK DRAKE

NICK DRAKE has published two collections of poetry: *The Man in the White Suit* (1999) won the Forward/Waterstone Prize for Best First Collection and was a Poetry Book Society Recommendation; *From the Word Go* appeared in 2007. He has also written a film, *Romulus, My Father*, starring Eric Bana and Franka Potente, which premiered in Australia in 2007 and won four AFI awards, including Best Film; it has since been released internationally. His stage adaptations include *To Reach the Clouds* (the story of Philippe Petit's audacious high wire walk between the Twin Towers in 1974), produced at Nottingham Playhouse in 2006, and *Stasiland*, based on the book by Anna Funder. He was an English undergraduate at Magdalene from 1980–83, studying under Richard Luckett and Arthur Sale.

IAN DUHIG

Ian Duhig was born into an immigrant family and worked with homeless people for fifteen years throughout England and Ireland before becoming a writer and poet. This is reflected in attitudes to home and landscape in his work, as suggested by the epigraph for his first book from Hugh of St Victor: 'The man who loves his homeland is a beginner; he to whom every soil is as his own is strong; but he is perfect for whom the entire world is a foreign country.' Duhig has written five books of poetry, most recently *The Speed of Dark* (Picador, 2007) which was shortlisted for the T. S. Eliot and Costa Poetry Prizes. More recently, a short story appeared in *The New Uncanny* (Comma, 2008) and the co-written *God Comes Home* about the legacy of David Oluwale was performed at the West Yorkshire Playhouse in February 2009.

JANE DURAN

Jane Duran was born in Cuba and brought up in the United States and Chile. Her collection *Breathe Now, Breathe* (Enitharmon, 1995) won the Forward Prize for Best First Collection. Enitharmon also published two subsequent collections: *Silences from the Spanish Civil War* (2002) and *Coastal* (2005). She received a Cholmondeley Award in 2005. The poems 'Morphology', 'The Andes' and 'Cordillera' are from her sequence 'Graceline', and the landscapes are Chilean.

ELAINE FEINSTEIN

Brought up in Leicester and educated at Newnham College, Cambridge, Elaine Feinstein has lived as a poet, novelist and biographer since 1980, receiving many awards, including a Cholmondeley Award for Poetry, an Honorary D.Litt. from the University of Leicester and a Rockefeller Foundation Fellowship at Bellagio. She received a major Arts Council award for her latest novel, *The Russian Jerusalem* (Carcanet, 2008). Her most recent book of poems is *Talking to the Dead* (Carcanet, 2007). In 2008 she was elected to the Council of the Royal Society of Literature. *Bride of Ice*, a new and extended selection of the poems of Marina Tsvetaeva, comes out in June 2009.

MATTHEW FRANCIS

MATTHEW FRANCIS is the author of four poetry collections, all of which explore landscape among other themes. In particular, *Whereabouts* (2005) consists of thirty-five short poems evoking various places at home and abroad, while his most recent collection, *Mandeville* (2008), describes the world from the point of view of the legendary medieval traveller Sir John Mandeville. His poetry has been shortlisted for the Forward Prize (twice) and for the Welsh Book of the Year Award, and he was named in 2004 as one of the Next Generation Poets. He is also the editor of the *New Collected Poems of W. S. Graham*, and has published a study of Graham, *Where the People Are*. His novel *WHOM* appeared in 1989, and current projects include a collection of short stories and a second novel. He is Reader in Creative Writing at Aberystwyth University.

JOHN GREENING

JOHN GREENING was born in 1954 in London. He has published twelve collections of poetry and received a Cholmondeley Award in 2008. *Hunts: Poems 1979–2009* appeared from Greenwich Exchange in Spring 2009. He has always been a 'poet of place' (Hounslow Heath, Upper Egypt, New Jersey, Iceland) and two of the three poems here pay close attention to a specific landscape, notably that undistinguished, overlooked scrubby patch of Englishness called Huntingdonshire—a county which doesn't even really exist any more. His abiding preoccupation with Polar regions (see the 2008 collection *Iceland Spar* from Shoestring Press) is reflected in the third poem, 'Ice Age'.

PHILIP GROSS

Apart from poetry, Philip Gross writes fiction for young people, plays, libretti and radio short stories. His adult poetry up to and including the Whitbread-shortlisted *The Wasting Game* is collected in *Changes of*

Address (Bloodaxe, 2001) followed by *Mappa Mundi* (2003), *The Egg of Zero* (2006) and later in 2009 *The Water Table*, which continues an investigation of place and landscape begun in *The Abstract Garden* (Old Stile Press, 2006), a book-length collaboration with engraver Peter Reddick. The new book centres on the shifting definitions of the Severn Estuary, where he now lives. Since 2004 he has been Professor of Creative Writing at Glamorgan University.

P. J. GRUBB

Professor PETER GRUBB is Emeritus Professor of Investigative Plant Ecology in Cambridge University. A Fellow of Magdalene College, he has carried out significant research in a very wide range of vegetation-types from tropical rain forest to desert, and has travelled extensively on all continents bar Antarctica. He is best known for his work on vegetational dynamics and especially the mechanisms whereby the co-existence of many species in a single plant community is maintained. Within Britain he has studied particularly the grasslands and scrub communities found on the chalk. Among numerous publications, he co-edited the *Journal of Ecology* from 1972 to 1977 and *Toward a More Exact Ecology* (1989), and was co-author of *100 Years of Plant Sciences in Cambridge 1904–2004*.

HAZEL HANCOCK (LAMBERT)

HAZEL HANCOCK (Lambert) is an artist with a keen interest in wildlife, wild creatures and natural landscapes. The backdrop to her own upbringing was the Hampshire Downs and Salisbury Plain: hedgehog-feeding and pond-dipping, nature walks in Harewood Forest, dabbling in the beautiful chalk streams of the Bourne Valley and Test Valley, with regular trips to the shores of north Cornwall for family holidays. Since graduating in Geography from Cambridge University in 2008, she has worked as an artist and photographer, as well as working to raise money for various charities.

NIGEL HAWKES

NIGEL HAWKES has taken many photographs of the buildings and grounds of Magdalene College, Cambridge, several of which are available to see on the College website. As computer officer, he has been closely involved in the Landscape Festival, and his image, Magdalene Tree, was used as the key image of the Festival.

M. E. J. HUGHES

Jane Hughes is a lecturer in English and has been a Fellow of Magdalene College, Cambridge, since 1987. She has written on parody and satire and is interested in the connections between medieval and contemporary writing. She is currently writing a history of satire and editing a twelfth-century book of advice to a young man about making his way in London. One of the directors of the Magdalene Festival, she plays a key role in opening up access to many of the intellectual resources of the College and of Cambridge to a wide range of people. She edited, with John Mole and Nick Seddon, the millennium volume *Figures of Speech: An Anthology of Magdalene Writers*.

JUDITH KAZANTZIS

Judith Kazantzis is an English–Irish poet and artist who lives in East Sussex. She has published nine books of poetry plus a midway *Selected Poems*. In 2007 she received the prestigious Cholmondeley Poetry Award. Recent collections include *Just after Midnight*; *Swimming through the Grand Hotel*; and *The Odysseus Poems: Fictions on the Odyssey*. Her next collection will be *Sister Invention*. Brought up among the oak spinneys of the Weald, she spent her first adult years discovering the South Downs, under the northern scarp of which is the elusive chalk monument 'The Long Man of Wilmington'. 'River that Flows Both Ways' is set in one of the regions of the US she has come to know well, the sombre summer forests and hills of the Hudson, whose place names still memorialise the dispossessed Native Americans. Website: www.judithkazantzis.com.

JOANNE LIMBURG

Joanne Limburg grew up in London and read Philosophy at King's College, Cambridge. Since then she has passed through the landscapes of Kent, mid-Lothian and Nottinghamshire, before returning first to London and then to Cambridge, where she now lives and is currently a Royal Literary Fund Writing Fellow at Magdalene College. She has published two books of poetry, *Femenismo* and *Paraphernalia* (Bloodaxe, 2000 and 2007) and has recently completed her first non-fiction book, *The Woman Who Thought Too Much*. Her poem for this anthology was inspired by an unexpected and disorienting encounter with the landscape of the American Mid-West, which looked altogether too much like it does in the films.

MICHAEL LONGLEY

Michael Longley was born in Belfast in 1939. After reading classics at Trinity College, Dublin, he taught in schools in Belfast, Dublin and London, joining the Arts Council of Northern Ireland in 1970 as Combined Arts Director. He was awarded the Queen's Gold Medal for Poetry in 2001 and the T. S. Eliot Prize in 2000. His poetry engages with the natural landscape and its wildlife in intimate detail, as well as presenting them as a counterbalance to the often violent contemporary urban world. His *Collected Poems* was published in 2006, and in 2007 he was appointed Professor of Poetry for Ireland.

ROD MENGHAM

Rod Mengham is Reader in Modern English Literature at the University of Cambridge, where he is also Curator of Works of Art at Jesus College. The author of *The Descent of Language* (1993) and of books on Charles Dickens, Emily Brontë, Henry Green and, most recently, Thomas Hardy, he is also editor of the 'Equipage' series of poetry pamphlets, co-editor and co-translator of *Altered State: the New Polish Poetry* (Arc, 2003) and co-editor of *Vanishing Points: New Modernist Poems* (Salt, 2005). His own poems have been published as *Unsung: New and Selected Poems* (Folio/Salt, 1996; 2nd ed., 2001); his latest collection is *Parleys and Skirmishes*, with photographs by Marc Atkins (Ars Cameralis, 2007). 'Grimspound' is an ongoing project, one of several concerning place and its representations, both in Britain and abroad, explored through a range of poetry and essays.

JOHN MOLE

John Mole's own blue remembered hills are the Quantocks where, as a boy, he explored the haunts of Wordsworth and Coleridge around Alfoxden and Nether Stowey, and he has always had a strong feeling for what the painter Paul Nash called 'charged landscapes'—the spirit of a particular place, whether rural or urban, and its challenge to the imagination. His poetry has received the Gregory and Cholmondeley Awards, and his writing for children the Signal Award. Books include *Counting the Chimes: New and Selected Poems 1975–2003* and *This is the Blackbird: Selected Poems for Children*. Most recently he has written the libretto for a community opera, *Alban*, performed in May 2009 in St Albans cathedral.

TOM MORIARTY

Tom Moriarty lives in Northamptonshire and is studying History at Magdalene College, Cambridge. He enjoys photographing flora and fauna, but his photograph in this volume, taken from above a car park, shows his interest in urban landscapes, as well as a fascination with unusual perspectives and angles. He tries to give most things he sees an opportunity to impress upon him their ability to look beautiful, given the right attention.

LES MURRAY

Les Murray was born in 1938 in Nabiac, a village on the north coast of New South Wales, Australia. A novelist as well as a poet, he has also edited a number of anthologies of Australian writings. Still living near to the dairy farm where he spent his childhood, Murray is deeply influenced and inspired by this evocative rural landscape of hills and forests. His collection *Subhuman Redneck Poems* (1996) won the T. S. Eliot Prize, and in 1998, the year his verse novel *Fredy Neptune* was published, he was awarded the Queen's Gold Medal for Poetry. His *New Collected Poems* came out in 2003 and *The Biplane Houses* in 2007, both published in the UK by Carcanet Press.

GREGORY NORMINTON

Gregory Norminton is a novelist and environmental activist living in Edinburgh. He was a Writer in Residence at Magdalene College, Cambridge, in 2006. He has published four novels, most recently *Ghost Portrait* and *Serious Things* (Sceptre, 2005 and 2008) which are much concerned with cultural and psychological responses to landscape. The four haiku from 'Malaysian Journal' were composed while filming the television series 'Planet Action' for Animal Planet: a six-part series exploring the work of WWF conservationists in various tropical countries. Website: www.gregorynorminton.co.uk

RUTH PADEL

Ruth Padel is a prize-winning poet, Fellow of the Royal Society of Literature and Zoological Society of London, formerly Chair of the Poetry Society and currently Resident Poet at Christ's College,

Cambridge. She has published seven collections of poetry, most recently *Darwin: A Life in Poems.* Her non-fiction includes a nature/travel book on wild tigers, much acclaimed for its description of Asian forest landscapes from Bhutan to Sumatra. The first section of *The Poem and the Journey*, her most recent book on reading contemporary poetry, turns on the landscape in which we find our first identity, and is prefaced by Viola's question in *Twelfth Night*, 'What country, friends, is this?' Website: www.ruthpadel.com.

IAN PATTERSON

IAN PATTERSON has worked in further education, and as a translator and a second-hand bookseller, and is now Fellow and Director of Studies in English at Queens' College, Cambridge. Among his books are *Guernica and Total War* (2007), a translation of Proust's *Le temps retrouvé*, *Time Found Again* (Penguin, 2003), and *Time to Get Here: New and Selected Poems* (Salt, 2003). His latest book of poetry, *The Glass Bell*, was published by Barque in 2009. Ideas and constructions derived from landscape have frequently shaped his work: his sequence 'Hardihood', for example, reassembled phrases from the poems of Thomas Hardy to create intellectually and affectively inflected landscape structures.

PASCALE PETIT

PASCALE PETIT has published four poetry collections including *The Huntress* and *The Zoo Father,* which were both shortlisted for the T. S. Eliot Prize and were books of the year in the *Times Literary Supplement*. Her latest collection is *The Treekeeper's Tale* (Seren, 2008) and, forthcoming from Seren in 2010, *What the Water Gave Me — Poems after Frida Kahlo*. The Poetry Book Society and Arts Council named her as one of the Next Generation Poets in 2004. She is widely travelled, including to coast redwood parks in California, the Venezuelan Amazon, Mexico, Kazakhstan, Nepal and China, where in 2007–8 she took part in the Yellow Mountain Poetry Festival on Huangshan in Anhui Province. She was the Royal Literary Fund Fellow at Middlesex University 2007-9 and tutors for The Poetry School and Tate Modern. Website: www.pascalepetit.co.uk.

JANE ROUTH

JANE ROUTH is a North Lancashire photographer and writer who looks after a flock of geese, an Ancient Semi-Natural Woodland, some new woods and a few fields. Her *Circumnavigation* (Smith/Doorstop, 2002) won the Poetry Business Competition and was shortlisted for the Forward Prize for Best First Collection. Her second book *Teach Yourself Mapmaking* (Smith/Doorstop, 2006) was a Poetry Book Society Recommendation, and was followed by a Templar Pamphlet *Waiting for H5N1* (2007), which explores the panic caused by the idea of avian influenza. She has lived for many years in the Forest of Bowland, and spends hours every day looking across fields and a deep river valley to the moors—a beautiful landscape but one shaped, like everywhere else, by its use (and abuse).

FIONA SAMPSON

Fiona Sampson lives in rural west Oxfordshire, an area susceptible to flooding. She has published fourteen books—poetry, philosophy of language and books on writing process—of which the most recent are: *Common Prayer* (2007, shortlisted for the T. S. Eliot Prize), *On Listening* (essays, 2007) and *Writing: Self and Reflexivity* (Macmillan, 2005). Her awards include the Newdigate Prize; 'Trumpeldor Beach' was shortlisted for the 2006 Forward Prize; and she has been widely translated, with eight books in translation, including *Travel Diary*, awarded the Zlaten Prsten (Macedonia, 2005). She contributes regularly to the *Guardian*, the *Irish Times* and other publications, and is the editor of *Poetry Review*.

DHANEESHA SENARATNE

A medical student at Magdalene College, Cambridge, Dhaneesha Senaratne was runner-up in the competition for the Magdalene Festival Art Prize with the image in this volume, showing a coastal scene in Sri Lanka. He is interested in depicting landscape through a range of photographic techniques including photomontage, and his imaginative use of shading makes his work particularly evocative.

NEIL WENBORN

Neil Wenborn is a full-time author and poet. He graduated from Magdalene College, Cambridge, and worked at the Bodleian Library in Oxford before pursuing a successful career in publishing. Since 1989 he has been a freelance writer and publishing consultant and has published widely both in Britain and in the United States. Recent works include biographies of Dvořák and Mendelssohn, and an e-book on Jane Austen's *Emma*. He is co-editor of the highly respected *Companion to British History* (Collins & Brown; Columbia University Press) and *A Dictionary of Jewish–Christian Relations* (Cambridge University Press). Landscape—especially the landscape of his adopted Fenland—has been a central focus of his poetry, a collection of which, *Firedoors*, is published by Rockingham Press.

SUSAN WICKS

Susan Wicks' first book of poems, *Singing Underwater* (Faber, 1992), won the Aldeburgh Poetry Festival Prize and was shortlisted for the Forward Prize for Best First Collection. Since then she has published four other collections of poetry, a collection of stories, two novels and a short memoir, *Driving My Father*. *The Clever Daughter* (1996) was a Poetry Book Society Choice and shortlisted for both Forward and T. S. Eliot Prizes. Her most recent book of poems, *De-iced*, came out from Bloodaxe in 2007. Her translation of *Pas Revoir*, a book-length sequence by the French poet Valérie Rouzeau, is due from Arc in 2009. Landscape and setting have played an increasingly important role in her work since *Night Toad: New & Selected Poems* (2003)—though landscape is always a focus for other themes and concerns.

CLIVE WILMER

Clive Wilmer is a poet, verse translator, critic and lecturer. He lives in Cambridge, where he is a Fellow of Sidney Sussex College, a Bye-Fellow of Fitzwilliam College and an Honorary Fellow of Anglia Ruskin University. His published work includes six volumes of his own poetry, the latest of which is *The Mystery of Things* (Carcanet, 2006). The earliest of the poems he keeps in print, 'The Ruined Abbey' (1965), was written in conscious tribute to William Wordsworth, the master of landscape poetry, and anticipates Wilmer's enthusiasm for another great writer on landscape, John Ruskin: he has made a study of Ruskin's work and is a Director of Ruskin's Guild of St George. Wilmer's own landscapes characteristically occupy the ambiguous borderland between the human built environment and the natural world.

TAMAR YOSELOFF

Tamar Yoseloff's poetry collections are *Sweetheart* (Slow Dancer, 1998), which was a PBS Special Commendation and the winner of the Aldeburgh Festival Prize, *Barnard's Star* (Enitharmon, 2004) and *Fetch* (Salt, 2007). She is also the author of Marks, a collaborative book with the artist Linda Karshan (Pratt Contemporary Art, 2007) and the editor of *A Room to Live In: A Kettle's Yard Anthology* (Salt, 2007). She is currently the poetry editor of *Art World* magazine and a tutor for The Poetry School in London. In 2005 she was Writer in Residence at Magdalene College, Cambridge, as part of the Year in Literature Festival. Desolate or ruined landscapes (in both urban and pastoral settings) have been a constant concern in her work.

ACKNOWLEDGEMENTS

'The Treasure Map': 'The Treasure Map' was first published in Ruth Padel, *Darwin: A Life in Poems*, published by Chatto and Windus, 2009.

'Betweenland': Acknowledgments are due to the editors of *SmartishPace*, where 'Betweenland' recently appeared in the USA.

'The Cowladder Stanzas': 'The Cowladder Stanzas' was first published in *Archipelago*.

'Morphology', 'The Andes': 'The Andes' was first published in *Magma*; 'Morphology' was first published in *Poetry London*.

'Deep Water': An earlier version of 'Deep Water' was first published in the *Warwick Review*.

'Cwm Elan': Thanks are due to the Powys Digital History Project for the information on their Elan Valley web pages: http://history.powys.org.uk/history/rhayader/elanmenu.html.

'The Transformation': 'The Transformation' was written for, and read at, the Poet in the City event 'Poetry and the Built Environment' (19 February 2008 at the German Gymnasium, St Pancras, London).

'Grimspound': An earlier selection of material from the project was exhibited in the Potocki Palace, Lviv, Ukraine, in 2005.

'Mist', 'Empire of After': 'Mist' and 'Empire of After' were first published in Nick Drake, *From the Word Go*, Bloodaxe Books, 2007.

'Enclosure Acts 1 & 2': Thanks are due to Gerry Bye for the reproductions of L. S. Bramwell's paintings.